THE ROAD
TO J.O.Y.

THE ROAD TO J.O.Y.

LEADING WITH FAITH, PLAYING WITH PURPOSE, LEAVING A LEGACY

SCOTT DREW

WITH DON YAEGER

W Publishing Group

An Imprint of Thomas Nelson

MAGNOLIA
PUBLICATIONS

Published in Nashville, Tennessee, by W Publishing, an imprint of Thomas Nelson.

Thomas Nelson titles may be purchased in bulk for educational, business, fundraising, or sales promotional use. For information, please email SpecialMarkets@ThomasNelson.com.

Published in association with Yates & Yates, www.yates2.com.

ISBN 978-0–7852-9168-8 (audiobook)
ISBN 978-0-7852-9167-1 (eBook)
ISBN 978-0-7852-9165-7 (HC)

Library of Congress Control Number: 2021953441

Printed in Canada

22 23 24 25 26 FRI 10 9 8 7 6 5 4 3 2 1

*To Jesus Christ, the one who makes it possible for
us to continue leading with faith, playing with
purpose, and hopefully, leaving a legacy.*

*To my wife, Kelly, and our children, Mackenzie, Peyton,
and Brody. I never could have done anything without
your constant encouragement and support.*

*To all the Baylor family who, for nineteen years, has faithfully and
loyally supported us and prayed for us, all to the glory of God.*

CONTENTS

CONTENTS

FOREWORD

Back in 2003 Jo and I were barely getting by. I guess you could look back and try and romanticize it by saying that we were "living simply," or just trying to scrape out a little piece of the American Dream like anyone else. But the truth is that we were hanging on for dear life. We had opened a little home decor shop called Magnolia here in Waco, all while trying to build a construction and home renovation business. By the state of things, I'd rolled the dice with our livelihood with no way of knowing how they were going to land.

But the most important things I felt I had figured out. I knew who I was and what mattered most. I was newly married to a woman I loved, who understood those same things about herself. We believed in each other, and we believed in a dream to build something that would matter—something that would be meaningful, not only to us, but to our families and our community. And who knows, maybe even the world. Imagine that. Two kids who could barely pay their bills thinking their dream could mean something. You can't say we lacked vision. Or the way I like to remember it—*belief.*

The part we couldn't yet see was how to bridge the gap between our *very real* reality and what we believed our little business, Magnolia, could be. And how we'd ever bridge that gap, we had no clue. Back then, the *how* seemed to be the most daunting part. But only in life's rearview mirror can we see that the real miracle is that we believed in this dream to begin with. The more life we live, the clearer it becomes to us that few people ever do. But we did! We believed in something that we felt in our souls was worth chasing. For better or for worse.

Just about the same time, on the other side of the interstate, a fresh-faced basketball coach named Scott Drew was being introduced at a Baylor press conference. He had just accepted what many people might have thought to be the worst job in the country.

The details are out there for everyone to see but suffice to say the Baylor basketball program was in a very difficult, if not impossible state in 2003. At a time when the program itself was in pieces, the game of basketball was the least of anyone's worries. This was going to take a rebuild from the ground up. Culture, character, philosophy—all the foundational elements had to be put in place before anybody even thought about lacing up their sneakers. What kind of coach would have the audacity to take a phone call for a job like that? For a position that was all but guaranteed to fail in the face of overwhelming national scrutiny?

Well, Scott Drew took the call.

Because he had something you can't always see on a resume: belief in something bigger than himself and the absolute will to stick it out until that belief became a reality. Like those two kids scraping by on the other side of town, he had a vision for something that seemed outright impossible.

A video of Coach Drew's first press conference all those years ago made the rounds last March when Baylor was closing in on their first national championship. With clear eyes and all the belief in the world, he said, "We came with the chance to win a national championship at Baylor University. We have the resources. We have the people. We have the leadership. And I think we have the family atmosphere to do it down here. And that's my goal in the next few years: to bring Baylor to that forefront."

His motivations were crystal clear. He planned to build something that would matter—not just for himself, but for the team, the community, and who knows, maybe even the world. And over the next eighteen years he stayed the course. He invested in the lives of young men who came and went. He poured into the Waco community. He changed what the world thought of Baylor basketball. And in March 2021 he led his team onto the court as green and gold confetti rained down. They were national champs! Just like he believed they would be, even if a "few years" turned into nearly two decades. But Coach Drew's legacy is bigger than winning a tournament.

Because his belief is big enough for all of us.

Over the years I've picked up on a few things when it comes to chasing something you believe in. And I'll say this: the pursuit of things like personal glory, wealth, success—that's shortsighted. You can't take any of that with you.

But when you run toward something bigger than yourself—all heart, no charade—and you turn that dream or idea outward, to lift others—that's the kind of thing that gets people running in the same direction. And one day you'll find that when you look to your left and look to your right, you're no longer running alone.

Because your belief was big enough for all of us.

Jo and I, and Coach Drew, we were all running in the same direction for a long while before we realized it. But I believe that his momentum contributed to ours, and hopefully that the same holds true the other way around.

So here's what we shouldn't forget: much of it started with a simple belief. Belief in something bigger than ourselves. And much of it stayed the course because a bunch of people chose to believe too. And I don't think it's because there was promise of glory in it or fanfare waiting on the other side.

Belief is enough. And Coach Drew is about the most qualified guy I know to tell you why.

Chip Gaines

ONE

SEE MOUNTAINS FROM VALLEYS

I can do all things through Christ who strengthens me.

PHILIPPIANS 4:13 (NKJV)

On the surface, it didn't make any sense. There I was, staring into the cameras and microphones during my introductory press conference, being announced as the new head coach at Baylor University. Just one month prior, I had been preparing to start my second year as a head coach at Valparaiso University, and my wife, Kelly, and I had moved into a new home we'd just built. We had also found out she was pregnant with our first child.

Now I was in a different state, literally and figuratively. I was in Waco, Texas, taking the head coaching job of arguably—because of a recent tragedy and scandal—the most infamous team in all of college sports.

The job had only become available three weeks before, and when it did, I felt like it could be the opportunity God was calling me to. Unlike Valparaiso, Baylor was in a major conference, which meant teams there had a chance to make the NCAA tournament on a regular basis and, eventually, compete for a national championship. That's what I saw and felt that God was calling us to.

But it wasn't the easiest decision.

In addition to what was happening in our own lives, the reality of what was happening in Waco would give anyone pause.

Baylor had started looking for a new coach in August of 2003 when Dave Bliss, the coach for the previous five seasons, had resigned in the wake of the ongoing national scandal.

In June of that year, one of their players, Patrick Dennehy, had gone missing. Baylor is the largest Baptist university in the country. I was coaching at Valpo, America's largest Lutheran school, and had worked in Christian coaching circles my entire, albeit young, career. So when the news of Baylor's missing player began to circulate, it made its way to my circle fairly quickly. My staff at Valpo started praying for Baylor and Patrick and his family, and we sent a letter to Coach Bliss offering our support.

Over the next several weeks, the situation in Waco only became more tragic.

Eventually, Patrick Dennehy's SUV was found in Virginia Beach, Virginia, which was near the hometown of one of Dennehy's teammates, Carlton Dotson, who was from Maryland.

On July 21 Dotson was arrested and charged with Dennehy's murder. Four days later, with Dotson's help, Dennehy's body was discovered in a gravel pit in Waco.

The school, town, and basketball world were shocked. Not only were people horrified at the idea that one teammate could murder another, but the reality that such a scandal could occur at Baylor made it all the more tragic. It became a national story, and the attention that it brought only exposed additional layers of brokenness.

On August 7 Patrick's friends and family held a funeral for him in his native San Jose, California. And on August 8 Coach Bliss resigned as the head coach at Baylor.

Just over a week after Bliss's resignation, the *Fort Worth Star-Telegram* reported on secret recordings of Coach Bliss made during meetings with some of his assistants. The recordings of those meetings revealed how Bliss was pushing his coaches to help him create the story that Dennehy, who was not on an official scholarship, was paying his way through school via drug sales. According to news reports, Bliss had more players on campus than available scholarships and so he was paying some of the players under the table to keep them around.

"What we've got to create here is drugs," one of the recordings had Bliss saying. "Our whole thing now, we can get out of it, okay? Reasonable doubt is there's nobody right now that can say we paid Patrick Dennehy, because he's dead."

There's a spiritual principle that says, "Everything you cover up God exposes. And everything you expose God covers up." To Baylor's credit, when they found out that the coaching staff was attempting to cover up previous misdeeds through falsehoods and accusations, they confronted the coaches and confessed the cover-up.

The fallout would eventually lead to the resignation of the athletic director. In August 2003, just two months before basketball practice would start, the school had no athletic director and no basketball coach. It also had a team faced with a devastated present and an uncertain future. The only thing anyone knew for sure about the future of Baylor basketball was that there would be stiff, possibly historic, sanctions from the NCAA.

Baylor and the NCAA granted all the players the ability to transfer. No one knew what the future would look like in Waco. They just knew it would be rough.

In the midst of all that, I was offered the Baylor job. Kelly and I kept praying about it and felt that, in spite of everything, this was what we were supposed to do.

Sometimes God calls us at the times when it doesn't seem to make much sense. So we have to rely on him and seek his hand in all of it.

Because of the scandal and the amount of national media attention it garnered, there were rows of reporters and TV crews present for the announcement that I was taking the job. You know how when there's a car crash, everyone slows down to take a look as they drive by? We had lots of people watching us.

The night before the press conference was actually the first time I'd ever set foot in Waco, let alone on Baylor's campus. I had no idea what I, along with my wife, family, and assistants, were walking into. But I knew we would be relying on God every step of the way. And when you do that, anything is possible.

> **I knew we would be relying on God every step of the way. And when you do that, anything is possible.**

The next morning I tried to cast a God-sized vision. As the leader, that was my job, to lay out what the goals were and how we would go about pursuing them. Who knew what was going to happen with any of it? But if we were moving our entire family and taking one of the most infamous jobs in America, we might as well give it our best shot. And if God had other plans for us, at least we could lay our heads down every night knowing we did our best. One of the things I've learned: always give 100 percent and let God decide the results. You don't want to go to bed with regrets. So don't hold back.

At the press conference, I didn't hold back.

In hindsight, I can see how, just two weeks after the previous coach resigned in shame, and facing an unknown amount of sanctions from the NCAA, it might have sounded naive, or crazy. But I wanted to share my heart and cast a vision for what we were coming to Waco to do.

"My goal at Valpo University was to be the first mid-major school to go to the Final Four in recent years," I began. "At Baylor University, I did not come to go to the NCAA tournament. We came to win games in the NCAA tournament. We came with the chance to win a national championship at Baylor University."

People thought I was nuts. But I wasn't trying to be bold or provocative. I was just saying what was on my heart. Why take the job if you don't think you can win?

The thing was no one had really been doing it. The team hadn't won an NCAA tournament game since 1950. But so what? So what if we would have reduced scholarships and limited chances for postseason play? As I said, "We have the resources. We have the people. We have the leadership. And I think we have the family atmosphere to do it down here."

More importantly, we had God.

I'd only been a head coach for one year, and probably only had that job because I was able to take over for my father. And Baylor might only have heard of me because of a famous moment that happened at our school a few years before. But so what? As the saying goes, God doesn't call the qualified, he qualifies the called.

I was all in, and I believed in our team and approach; and I knew a mighty God could do all things. So it was easy for me to say, in full faith and calm clarity, that winning a national championship was possible.

Even if I didn't quite realize yet how mighty God was going to need to be, I was ready for this next phase of the journey. And now I can see with a grateful and humble heart how God had been preparing me for it my entire life.

TWO

YOU ARE FORMED FROM THE BEGINNING

"For I know the plans I have for you," declares the LORD, "plans to prosper you and not to harm you, plans to give you hope and a future."

JEREMIAH 29:11

When you are faced with a challenge or difficult decision, sometimes it can be helpful to ask yourself, How am I uniquely equipped to handle this situation? What has God done in my life to prepare me for this moment? What experiences, positive or negative, have I faced that have strengthened me for the battle ahead? What people has God put in my life to help form me into the person who's ready for what's next?

I wouldn't have been ready to take on a challenge like the Baylor job if God hadn't put some incredible people in my life. Specifically, my family.

Like most people, my earliest childhood memory involves my parents. Specifically, it involves my father, Homer. And, technically, the police. I can remember it was late at night, and I was lying down in the front seat of our car as my father drove us through the night. You couldn't do it today because we have car seats and seatbelt laws. But back then you could lie down in the front seat with your head in your father's lap, with the hum of the road under the tires that just seems so comforting. The next thing I remember was the lights. And the sirens.

Apparently, my father's enthusiasm for recruiting exceeded the state of Louisiana's tolerance for speeding, which a police officer was kindly discussing with my dad. As a kid, seeing the police car with the flashing lights was really fun. I have since come to find out that my father didn't exactly feel the same way. The next thing I remember, we were leaving the state.

We were living in Baton Rouge, Louisiana, because my dad was working as an assistant on Dale Brown's staff at LSU. Growing up in St. Louis, my dad's first real coaching job in college basketball was in Pullman, Washington, as an assistant at Washington State University. Dale Brown had been an assistant on that team, and when the coach at Washington State, Bob Greenwood, resigned after the first season, that left Dale and my dad without jobs.

Luckily, Coach Brown was able to get the job as head coach at LSU. He brought my dad, my mom, Janet, and me to join him. I was all of two years old, and Coach Brown offered my dad the ultimate extra benefit: his daughter Robyn could babysit me when needed.

I can't imagine the pressure my dad must have felt, moving his family across the country for a new job, as well as the pressure to recruit and help Coach Brown build LSU's program. Coach Brown had this insane energy, traveling day and night all over the state, handing out basketball nets anywhere he went, kissing every baby he could, and holding camps for kids as a way of reminding the residents that the Louisiana State Tigers played basketball as well as football. As his lead assistant, my dad had to work as hard, if not harder, than Coach Brown. That's one of the first things I learned from my dad: there is no shortcut for hard work. It takes time, it takes energy, and it takes effort. My dad always had ample supplies of energy and effort. But in Baton Rouge, our family of three turned into a family of five when my sister, Dana, and later my brother, Bryce, were born. Time became precious. But my dad was trying his best.

I was in the car with my dad on that drive when he was pulled over because bringing me on recruiting trips was an opportunity to spend time with me. LSU was in the Southeastern Conference and, while the school wasn't known for basket-ball, Coach Brown was selling his vision.

> **There is no shortcut for hard work. It takes time, it takes energy, and it takes effort.**

And my dad was with him every step of the way. But with me, Dana, and Bryce all under the age of six, my dad saw a different vision. He saw one where he was home more with us and my mom, where he was as involved in coaching us in life as he was in coaching any of his players in basketball. He had to make a choice between putting more of his energy into his career or taking a job that would allow more time for his family. Ultimately, he chose us. So in the summer of 1976, our family loaded up a U-Haul and left big-time college athletics for tiny Bethel College in northern Indiana. He was leaving a good job as a lead assistant at a big school in a major conference in the NCAA for a head coaching job at a small school that wasn't even a part of the NCAA. I didn't realize it at the time but, looking back, he was giving up the pursuit of the promises of the world to provide for the family he'd been given.

My last night in Louisiana, like a lot of summer nights in Louisiana, was incredibly hot. And, like a lot of families back then, we didn't have air conditioning. I was hopeful that this new place we were going, if nothing else, would at least have air conditioning. After a day of driving, we stopped for the night and we three kids all slept on the floor of the hotel. Finally, two days after leaving Baton Rouge, we arrived in Mishawaka, Indiana.

Mishawaka is a twin city of South Bend, Indiana, home to the prestigious Notre Dame Fighting Irish. While Bethel College was a private Christian school near Notre Dame, the reality couldn't have been further from the truth. Which is exactly how my dad wanted it. My dad wasn't just the coach at Bethel College. He was the athletic director and a professor. I mention that only to highlight what life was like in a small college like Bethel. You had to work very hard and wear various hats. But when I think about my dad and our time with him in Bethel College, I don't think about him in an office or in a classroom. I think about him in the gym.

The gym at Bethel was like a big high school gymnasium. But for me, at six years old, it was the world's greatest playground. In addition to the basketball court, the gym had an auditorium, which meant a stage, which we turned into our Wiffle ball stadium. Basic rule: if you hit it onto the stage, it was a home run. We played everything in that gym—football, tag, and basketball. Some of my friends had tree forts in their backyards. Some people had jungle gyms. We had Bethel College's gymnasium. It shaped our childhood and, in the process, our lives.

Now, my dad had taken a low-profile job with a fraction of the pressure by going to Bethel. But he still had a job. And, if you've ever met my dad, you know he still worked incredibly hard. He still had to go and recruit players and coach games. But at a smaller school there was more of an opportunity for us to wear some of those hats. I would be able to go with my dad on some of his recruiting trips (this time from the back seat). And I would be able to go to most of his games, even helping him keep the team statistics. Sometimes when he had a late game away from home, I'd fall asleep on the couch waiting for him to come home—sometimes at 2:00 a.m. I can remember asking him, "Did we win?" and then going to my own bedroom. So it's fair to say I was heavily involved in my dad's coaching career, even though he had taken a smaller job. But that wasn't all I was doing—not by a long shot.

My dad may have taught basketball, but he was our life coach. Along with my mom, he had us participating in every activity you could think a kid could be in. It's probably not surprising that my sister, brother, and I all ended up in basketball. But it wasn't for a lack of exposure to other things. We did karate, tennis, baseball, football, piano, and even took guitar lessons. The cool part was that we experienced different sports and music and saw what we liked. My problem was I liked basketball. But I was short. I was so short my mom had to sew my uniforms just so I could wear them. As a five-foot-two sophomore in high school, unless you are someone like Muggsy Bogues, you aren't going to have much of a future playing basketball, regardless of who your father is. And, as I was often reminded, I wasn't Muggsy Bogues.

The good news is that God's plan is always best. Would I have liked to have been taller? Absolutely. If I had been taller, would I have been good enough to get a scholarship to a big school? Absolutely not. Realistically, I may have been good enough to be a Division II or Division III player. Luckily, God is in charge. At my height, I chose a sport with a net a lot closer to the ground—I played tennis. More importantly, I chose a school not based on where I would be able to play basketball. And I'm so glad I did.

By my senior year of high school, my dad had started a new job as the head coach at a small Lutheran Division I school, Valparaiso University. About sixty miles west of Mishawaka, Valparaiso was also the name of the town where the school is located. And, truthfully, I could have gone to Valpo University to play tennis. I wasn't Jimmy

Connors or Björn Borg, but I did start to grow (a little) and, for a small guy, I was a problem on the tennis court.

Instead, I went to Butler University about two and a half hours south in Indianapolis. And while I gave being the Indiana version of Jimmy Connors a shot by playing on the tennis team, my future was on a different court. I had started working summer camps for LSU and Notre Dame, as well as for my father for the middle and high school players in the area. Working those camps helped shape my future as a coach in two key areas: I learned how to teach the game of basketball, and I learned how to sell. I learned to teach basketball because in the camps you are just doing drills and practices all day long. It's one thing to watch your dad coach in practices and games. But when you get to run your own drills and offer your own instruction, it's like going from watching someone drive to sitting in the driver's seat. And I liked to drive.

When I say working the camps taught me how to sell, I mean it literally. In addition to working the camps as a coach, I was also working the concession stands and convincing the kids to buy candy or the hot dogs my mom made. If you can't sell candy to a teenager, maybe being in the persuasion business isn't for you.

The summer camps, plus coaching my brother's and sister's teams as they grew up, were a great introductory experience to coaching, but my time at Butler was an amazing next step in my journey. And that's why I can look back and thank God for keeping me so short. If I was taller, I might have gone somewhere else to college to play ball. Instead, I learned how to be a coach at Butler. Partly because of my father, I was able to get a student assistantship on Barry Collier's staff with the Bulldogs. Butler was a Division I team beginning to build a great program. And on Coach Collier's staff were amazing coaches, like Jay John and Thad Matta, who both went on to become outstanding head coaches in their own right. They took me under their wings and poured into me in ways they didn't have to. So now I had a father who had mentored me and a couple seasons as a student assistant doing any and every job the coaching staff didn't want, which gave me exposure to basketball at a level I hadn't seen before. And really, what it added up to was a problem.

The plan had been for me to graduate from Butler and then go to law school. And when I say "the plan," this was my dad's plan. Well, after the Christmas break before I graduated, I realized I didn't want to do that. I wanted to coach. I don't know what it was like for my dad to hear that, but I know that he told me to do what he always tells me to do when a tough decision is at hand—pray. I prayed and I wrote letters. Lots of letters. I wrote letters to any coach I could think of who might have a spot on their staff where I could work after I graduated. Once again, God answered my prayers in a way that I didn't anticipate or really even like at first.

The thing about coaching is that it's really hard to get your foot in the door. And when you haven't played college basketball, it's even harder. I sent out all those letters trying to get on a staff. Coaching staffs were a lot smaller then, and there were restrictions about grad-

> **God answered my prayers in a way that I didn't anticipate or really even like at first.**

uate assistant spots, so I didn't get many responses. The ones I did get weren't positive. I call them "ding letters," which basically means, "Hey, thanks for your interest, but we don't have a spot."

I really appreciated all the coaches who took the time to tell me they didn't have an opening. Today, I always try to respond to people if I can, even if it's with disappointing news. So I was striking out at every turn but still felt like I was called to coach. As it turns out, I got some help from two familiar faces.

That spring, my dad had his old boss Dale Brown visit to speak to his team at Valparaiso. By this point, Coach Brown had been to several Final Fours and had successfully recruited a bunch of top high school players to LSU, including Shaquille O'Neal, who was the previous year's top pick in the NBA draft.

When Coach Brown was speaking, I was in the room, and he pointed at me and told my dad, "You gotta hire the young kid." Around the same time, my dad's staff had an opening for a graduate-level position. For $600 a month and the ability to earn my master's degree, I took a job on my dad's staff.

Now, at $600 a month, I wasn't exactly living large. I was living at home with my parents and barely making any money. But you know what? I loved it.

First, thanks to my mom, I did have a solid meal plan. And, since I didn't have any money to do things, I just worked all the time. I basically lived at the office. At my first meeting with my dad's staff, I told them, "Give me everything you don't want to do."

I think God's allowing me to be humbled by starting at the bottom, living at home, doing the most menial tasks was one of the best blessings I could receive. Since I was low man on the totem pole, I had total freedom to try to recruit the best players I could find since there wasn't any pressure on me to land anyone. That time helped me develop this idea of starting at the top and working down in terms of the players I was recruiting, instead of the other way around. As a coach, if you only get who you could or should, it's going to keep you where you are, not where you are trying to be. And I was trying to help my dad take his team to the top.

That's the other thing working for my dad taught me. When you're coaching for your dad, you feel like a head coach. Because when your dad gets criticized in the media, when you lose a game, you take it like a head coach, if not more personally. When it happens to you, it's one thing. But when it happens to a parent or a sibling, it makes you more upset. When I was coaching with my dad, I took the losses and criticism harder than my father did. And I tried to help in any way I could—coach harder in practice, recruit harder on the phone—to try to protect my dad. When you're an assistant coach working for someone else, you care. But it's not your record and it's not your name. I'm glad God gave me the opportunity to work hard for my dad's name.

Above all, the biggest thing I learned from my dad is that, no matter what was happening in his life, no matter what was happening with his team, his faith in and relationship with God never wavered. He knew, and taught us, that God was good no matter who won or lost a game. And I can see now, with the benefit of my own age and maturity, how his faith helped guide him throughout his career. When he was at LSU, the NCAA rules really made it tough to have a family, especially if you were a worker, because you were allowed to be on the road recruiting literally all the time. And if you were building something, you'd have to work. As I was emerging as an assistant coach on his staff, it helped me realize just how much he sacrificed. He was on the verge of becoming a head coach and he gave that up for us. But I also realized that, in doing so, he propelled me and my siblings into our own careers.

Often you hear kids that resent what their parents do because they don't like what that made their parents become. Some people who had alcoholic parents, for example, don't want anything to do with alcohol, right? They don't like what that made their parents do. Well, it's similar for coaches' kids. Some of them don't want to go into the profession because they resent the impact that profession had on their own childhoods. To me, one of the greatest signs of respect a son could show his father is to follow in his footsteps, because that means he really admires his dad. I'm eternally grateful to my father for many things, but not the least is how his sacrifice has been redeemed in part by my own journey and that of my brother, Bryce, and my sister, Dana.

Even when it might seem like it's causing you to let go of something important, what God has for you is always better than anything you can get for yourself.

And it's in my father's story that I'm reminded, once again, about how great God is and to always trust his plan and his timing. Even when it might seem like it's causing you to let go of something important, what God has for you is always better than anything you can do on your own. Because while my dad did walk away from the spotlight of big-time college basketball in pursuit of a faith- and family-centered life, the spotlight still found him.

THREE

YOU ARE FORGED
BY STRENGTH

Iron sharpens iron, and one man sharpens another.

PROVERBS 27:17 (ESV)

Some people have asked me if winning a national championship will make it harder to stay humble, and others have asked if it will make it tougher to remain focused. And I get it. When you get put on a pedestal by the world, sometimes it can be easy to think you deserve to be there because of what you did, not what God did through you. In his providence, God has prepared me for making sure I never make things about myself. He made my younger brother Bryce Drew.

> **When you get put on a pedestal by the world, sometimes it can be easy to think you deserve to be there because of what you did, not what God did through you.**

You probably know Bryce. His senior year at Valpo University, he hit one of the most iconic shots in college basketball history. It

17

gets replayed over and over every March during the NCAA tournament. He's famous. A few months after we won the title game against Gonzaga, I was on the road recruiting. I was taking a taxi back to my hotel, and when I handed the driver my credit card, he looked down at my name.

"Scott Drew . . ." he said as his voice trailed off. "I know a Bryce Drew. He hit that famous shot."

I just smiled and took my card back. The Bible is full of stories of brothers having broken relationships because of jealousy. Cain killed Abel because the Lord regarded Abel's offering over his own. Jacob and Esau fought after Jacob tricked Esau into forfeiting his birthright. Joseph's older brothers sold him into slavery.

I can proudly say that I've never been tempted to sell Bryce into slavery. I've never really been anything but proud of him. The reality is, God's plan for our lives includes the people he puts in them. And looking back, I can see how Bryce's path and accomplishments have only served to shape my own.

Growing up, Bryce and I were competitive in the best way brothers could be. By that, I mean I won at most things. I was four years older, so I was just far enough ahead to keep us from being too physical or inappropriate whenever a game of Ping-Pong or one-on-one basketball started getting out of hand. But I was also five-foot-two, so once Bryce started growing, it was clear he would be able to reach both literal and figurative heights as a basketball player that I couldn't.

By the time he started high school, I was in college at Butler, so I kept up with his development from afar. And he did develop. As a coach's son he obviously had a lot of access to gyms and coaching. But he grew to be six foot three, and his physical development, paired with his work ethic, allowed him to make the most of his opportunity. By his senior year, he had become one of the best players in the state and would be named "Mr. Basketball" in Indiana, the most prestigious award in the state for a high school player. After I graduated from Butler and joined Dad's team as an assistant, it became clear we had one main recruit we were trying to land. And we happened to share a hallway bathroom.

Recruiting your brother can be a weird thing. You want to support him and see him do the best he can. You also want your dad to do the best he can, which sort of depends on landing your brother to be on his team. And as a young coach, you want to prove to your boss, who happens to be your father, that you can add value as a recruiter. So the breakfast table can have a lot more on it than just the juice and waffles.

But rather than focus on the potential awkwardness or obstacles of recruiting my younger brother, I saw it as a blessing and an opportunity. Back then, coaches would call your house to talk to a player. This may be hard for some people to believe, but we used to have phones wired into our homes. And we had phones in most rooms. So when coaches would call our house to talk to Bryce, I would listen in on the other line—with Bryce's permission of course. What I heard was a crash course in how to recruit—how to talk to players, connect with them, lay out a vision for your team and that player's role on it. And since Bryce had become one of the best players in the state, I heard from the top coaches in the country.

Imagine hearing Steve Jobs talk about how to create or market a product. Or Billy Graham talk about how to pray or construct a sermon. Or Denzel Washington talk about how to prepare for an acting role. That's how it was for me—I was hearing from the top people in the country in the field I wanted to be in. It was like a private lesson—for free. Even better, I was hearing what the competition was doing to sell my brother on playing for them. So when I wrote my own letters to Bryce—yes, I wrote my brother letters to try to convince him to go to the school my dad and I worked at—I was able to be as informed as possible about what else he was hearing.

In the end, Bryce chose to stay close to home. Literally. When he committed to play for Dad at Valpo, it was like we felt this switch turn on, and the status of our program would only go up. With Bryce committed, we could attract better players and sell them on the idea that we had a chance to do special things. And over the next four years of Bryce's career, that's exactly what happened.

With Bryce on the team, we started winning in unprecedented ways. His freshman year we won the conference for the first time ever but didn't earn an automatic bid to the NCAA tournament because our league didn't have one that year. That changed when, in his sophomore and junior seasons, we won the conference regular seasons and tournaments, qualifying for the "Big Dance" for the first time in the school's, and my dad's, history.

By 1998, Bryce's senior season, we were clearly the best team in the conference, and ready to do something bigger. We had narrowly lost our NCAA tournament game in 1997 against Boston College and were blown out the season before by Arizona.

As a small conference school, we knew we would be a lower-seeded team and would match up against a much larger school from a major conference. No matter who we faced, we would be clear underdogs. On paper, at least.

When the March Madness bracket was revealed, we were listed as a No. 13 seed, matched up with No. 4 seed Mississippi from the Southeastern Conference. Nicknamed Ole Miss, the Rebels had won their division that year, were ranked thirteenth in the country at the end of the season, and were led by Ansu Sesay, their 6–9 conference player of the year.

We were led by Bryce, who as a senior was the two-time Mid-Continent Conference player of the year. As his brother, I was so proud of him. As an assistant coach, I knew how good he was and that, as long as he was on, we had a chance against anyone.

The game was back and forth throughout, with Ole Miss having the lead most of the game but us hanging in there, giving us a chance at the end. When they missed a contested layup with seventeen seconds to go, we had the ball and trailed by two points. My dad didn't call time-out or signal in a play. He didn't need to. Everyone knew we wanted to get the ball to Bryce. Dribbling up the court, he picked up his dribble to shoot from outside, but he had a man in his face blocking his view. Bryce quickly passed to an open man just outside the three-point arc; sprinted past the defender, who turned his head; and caught the ball in space just outside the three-point arc He rose to shoot an open three with seven seconds left that would have put us up by one. I watched the ball in the air, thinking it was going to go in.

It hit the front rim and bounced off, into the arms of Ansu Sesay, who grabbed it and was fouled with 4.1 seconds to go.

As his brother, I was disappointed to see what could have been Bryce's last shot in college be one that came up short. Two years prior, we had nearly upset Boston College in the NCAA first round. And nothing really validates you as a player, or a coach if you're at a small school, like winning a game in the NCAA tournament. As a son, and brother, I wanted that so badly for my family.

As a coach, I was hoping we could get lucky with Sesay's free throws because if he made both of them, it would have effectively ended the game.

The first free throw missed, which meant no matter what, we would have a chance to tie the game. The crowd, sensing that there was still some basketball meat left on the bone, started making more noise.

Unbelievably, Sesay missed the second free throw, and after a brief scramble, the ball went out of bounds with 2.5 seconds left. The officials said it was our ball, still down only two.

With no time-outs left, we didn't have time to huddle up or draw a play. Luckily, we all knew what to do. My dad had drilled into us exactly the play we needed for moments like this. We knew what we were going to do. We knew we were going to go back to Bryce. The fact that he had just missed an open three-pointer didn't make us hesitant to go back to him. If anything, it made us feel like his next shot was more likely to go in. Bryce worked so hard all the time and had proven capable of these moments over and over. One stumble didn't deter us.

The play was called "Pacer," after the NBA team in Indianapolis. It was one we had practiced throughout the season.

The play started with senior guard Jamie Sykes inbounding the ball from underneath our own basket, ninety-four feet from where we needed to end up. Now, the thing about Jamie—he's only five foot eleven. Typically, you have taller people throw the ball inbounds for last-second shots because their height allows them to see over the defender, so they can see more of the court, and it is easier for them to find the open man. So Ole Miss's coaches might have been surprised to see one of our shortest guys throwing the ball inbounds. What they might not have known is that not only was Jamie a very good passer (he ended up finishing sixth all-time at Valpo for assists), but he was also an excellent baseball player. He had been drafted by the Arizona Diamondbacks the previous summer to play professional baseball as an outfielder. He had a very good arm.

Of course, with Bryce being our best player, defenses would naturally be paying him extra attention, probably with an extra defender. That's why my dad designed the play Pacer. We ran it all the time in practice, always at the end, when we were tired and wanted to go home.

Jamie took the ball from the referee. Ole Miss decided to guard the inbounds player, leaving Bryce with a single defender. Bill Jenkins, our six-foot-six forward who had been guarding Sesay all game, ran toward the top of our three-point arc. Now, for a college forward, being six foot six isn't really that tall. Especially when you're going up against

All-Conference guys. But Bill's first passion wasn't basketball—it was volleyball. That meant that Bill was excellent at jumping straight in the air from a set position. So once Bill got to his spot, and Jamie's pass was exactly where we planned it, Bill rose in the air to get the pass. Once it became clear the pass wasn't going to Bryce, the defense's eyes went toward the ball—and Bill.

Bill caught the ball at the height of his jump, with several Ole Miss defenders around him. But instead of coming down with the ball, he flicked his wrists to the left while still in midair, into the path of a streaking Bryce, who was suddenly wide–open. Bryce caught the ball just outside the three-point arc, right in front of our bench, with me and our dad watching on.

What happened next, I'm happy to say, is literally the stuff of legends.

The shot went in, and one of the most iconic moments in March Madness history was born. We all went crazy, hugging and jumping all over the court. Bryce had slid onto the court, and we all kind of dogpiled on top of him.

I can't really describe the mix of emotions happening at that moment. You're thrilled as a competitor that you won the game. You're even happier that your brother had this incredible moment to celebrate all that he'd accomplished in his career. And you are humbled by the idea that your father, who has worked so hard and sacrificed so much to provide for us in a way that allowed him to be a part of our lives, had a signature win for his career, and ministry.

There's no doubt that Bryce's shot helped elevate the profile of Valpo's program, and the nation couldn't help but eat up the whole "son hits the winning shot on his father's team" story line. It was *Hoosiers* meets David versus Goliath, only if Goliath had been holding David's dad hostage.

Today, in my office, I have a picture of that moment, nicknamed

"The Shot." It's a picture of Bryce elevating with the ball in his hands while our entire bench, including Dad and me, watch on.

But the thing about that picture is, that image isn't about the 2.5 seconds when the Pacer play was executed. That picture is about our childhood and how we were raised. That picture is about our lives as a coach's kids, and all the summers we spent at summer camps, and the time we spent in gyms just playing around. And goofing off while Dad was working with a player or on things in his office. That picture is about us moving as a family so Dad could take a different job, which of course impacted our entire lives. It's about Bryce's development and recruitment as a player, which helped shape me as a coach, him as a player, and us as a team.

It's about all the practices we shared as a family, with Dad as coach, me as an assistant, and Bryce as the player who worked so hard to become the best player in program history. And it's about those four years together, along with the rest of the team, working, sweating, sacrificing, and sharing, all for the hope of a greater good that may or may not be realized on the court. That picture was about Jamie and Bill and the rest of the team running that play in practice over and over, even though we never knew for sure if we would need it. Most importantly, that picture is about God taking all of it, and all of us, our family both in blood and in basketball, and doing a thing greater than we ever might have hoped. At Valpo, it was really hard to win a national championship. But you can win the national attention. Getting to a Sweet 16 got us exactly that. And that picture is about how, for a moment, this group of kids from a small town in Indiana was able to do just that.

> **The best part is that our story didn't end in that moment. It only got better.**

The best part is that our story didn't end in that moment. It only got better.

24

That window was big for our team, undoubtedly. But it was even bigger for our family. My dad was now a household name. And so was Bryce. Looking back, I can see how Bryce's shot elevated the profile of not only the Valparaiso brand but also the Drew family name. When I interviewed with Baylor, I wasn't just the Valpo coach. I was Homer's son. I was the assistant on the team that upset Ole Miss and the brother of the guy who made that famous shot. Bryce's shot changed our entire family's trajectory, not the least of which is my own. Who can be jealous about that?

Now, I didn't get the Baylor job because of *that*. But I got the interview.

I think I got the job because, even at a young age, I had carved out a reputation as a pretty good recruiter. I even won a national award for being good in that area. Bryce was a major reason why. But he also had another connection to my taking the Baylor job.

After his college career ended, Bryce was good enough that he was actually drafted as the sixteenth pick in the first round to play in the NBA by the Houston Rockets. I can't tell you what it's like to now be the big brother of an NBA player, someone who now shares a locker room with future NBA Hall of Famers like Charles Barkley, Scottie Pippen, and Hakeem Olajuwon. A lot of guys would let that status, and the seven-figure contract they signed as an NBA first-round pick, change them or go to their heads. But not Bryce.

Barkley told me a story recently about a road trip the Rockets were taking during Bryce's rookie season. They were flying to their city after a game, and the team plane started having some turbulence, so much so that not only was the plane wobbling an uncomfortable amount, but the air masks also dropped down from the overhead compartments. Never one to miss a moment for levity, Barkley announced to the team, before putting his mask on, "I don't know about the rest of you, but me, Bryce, and Brent [Price] are going to heaven."

I love so many things about that story, not least of which is that Charles was still devoted to God even in a potentially stressful moment when some might be losing their minds. But also that Bryce's faith was still so clear even as he became greater in the world. That's Bryce. He made a famous shot in college, but he wanted to be known for so much more than that, and he made it a point every day to be much more than that. And he was.

After two seasons in Houston, Bryce was traded to the Chicago Bulls, where he played for a coach named Tim Floyd. Floyd had come from Iowa State, a college team in the Big 12—the same conference that Baylor is in. As a longtime college coach, he also knew my father. Those Bulls teams were the first ones after Michael Jordan and Phil Jackson retired. To put it gently, they were rebuilding. But because Bryce was on the team, I got to know Coach Floyd that season, and Coach Floyd would be the one who called me the following year, encouraging me to think about taking the Baylor job.

After his playing career was over, Bryce did what any good Drew man does: he became a coach at Valpo under our father. After five years, he became the head coach. And now, instead of my learning how to be a good recruiter by listening in on his phone calls, he was calling me for advice.

I love that as Bryce was starting his coaching career, I could be the one to help him, giving advice on the importance of good assistants, or the way you want to set up your team's schedule, or just how to balance being a husband and father while running a team. Of course, Bryce doesn't need all that much help from me on that—we both had a pretty great mentor.

Trust me—I could have been jealous about Bryce's superior height, talent, and accomplishments as a basketball player. Joseph's brothers certainly were jealous of him. But I think one thing our father, and our faith, taught us is to see God in all of it. And if you can do that, then it will make you appreciative for all the blessings, and people, in your life. Joseph's brothers eventually recognized the error in their sin, repented, and were blessed by God through Joseph as a result. One thing I've learned is that God will prevail no matter what, but it's a whole lot easier if you just trust him to be in charge earlier rather than later.

I'm so thankful for Bryce, and I'm humbled by the ways God has allowed his ability and path to help shape my own. Because of Bryce's shot, the entire college basketball world knew our names. I'm honored to have an opportunity to use my name to make more people know God's.

FOUR

TAKE FIRST STEPS BOLDLY

"I know your works. Behold, I have set before you an open door, which no one is able to shut. I know that you have but little power, and yet you have kept my word and have not denied my name."

REVELATION 3:8 (ESV)

Some people may be surprised to find that the phrase "When one door closes, another opens" isn't actually in the Bible. But I think the concept of God opening doors he wants you to walk through is biblical. And, sometimes, you only find your way there because you suddenly discover that the path you thought you were supposed to be on has ended. Or at least doesn't go where you thought it would.

But the more you're in touch with God, the easier it can be to trust him and to discern the doors he wants you to walk through.

After Bryce left Valparaiso for the NBA, I continued on what I was sure was my path by working as an assistant for my dad, helping the team, and making a name for myself by bringing in some really good recruits. Thankfully, that talent we were bringing in kept the team successful on the court. We made the NCAA tournament three of the next four years, though we never did pull off any other upsets.

The year after Bryce went to the NBA, while I was still working with my father, I started to feel like I was ready to start my own family. The one thing my parents told me consistently growing up about dating or courting was that they prayed I would choose a Christian wife. So, in April of 1999, after the end of the college basketball season, I got serious about trying to do that. I didn't sign up for any dating websites (they didn't even exist then!) or start going out at night. I just started praying and asked God to let me meet a Christian woman who I might be able to marry.

One month later, I met Kelly.

Kelly was in law school at Missouri with our cousin Jill and had actually known Bryce for a while. But when I met her, I felt like she was a total five star—the kind of wife the Bible says we all should seek in Proverbs 31. She was kind, incredibly intelligent, beautiful, and was a leader in the Christian community in her school. Suddenly, my idea of recruiting who you wanted instead of who you thought you could get seemed like it would pay off.

Kelly was living in Missouri, and I was in Indiana, so it was a long-distance recruitment. But it wasn't casual. I called her all the time. Like, all the time.

She had grown up with two big basketball fans as parents, so I think being in the sport was sort of fun for her. And, as we got to know each other, God worked it out. We were married the following year.

That's one of the reasons having faith is pretty easy for me. When God gives you a wife like Kelly, it's not hard to trust him in many other ways.

Having a son who was married and settled down, my dad may have sensed that I might be ready for something more. After the 2002 season, when we lost to Kentucky by fifteen in the first round of the

NCAA tournament, my dad announced he was stepping down, and it was decided that I would replace him. Looking back, it is obvious he wasn't ready to step down. But he chose loving and supporting his family over his own career. What a role model.

At the time, I had some awareness of my father giving me the opportunity, but I was probably as eager to get going as I was appreciative of what he had done. And one of the things he did, after stepping down, was give me space to run the program in a way that made it my own. I know some churches have a hard time if a new pastor comes in and the former one sticks around, and it can be tough if the former pastor isn't intentional about receding into the background. My dad stayed away unless I asked him to come around, which was another way he sacrificially loved me and the team.

I hired Mike Heideman to be my top assistant coach, and at age fifty-four he became the elder statesman of the staff. Mike had been at Wisconsin Green Bay with Dick Bennett, and he brought a lot of experience that was really nice to have in the absence of my dad. But I still called Dad a lot too.

We had a really good team coming back, but we also had a really good recruiting class coming in. Everyone was excited for not only that year but also for that following year as well.

Our first game that season couldn't have been any tougher: at Syracuse, in the Carrier Dome, against legendary coach Jim Boeheim and an All-American recruit, Carmelo Anthony. Still, walking into one of the biggest and most famous arenas in college basketball for my first game as a head coach was pretty cool. When the game started, it got even cooler.

We started out hot, made some three-pointers over the famous zone defense that Syracuse plays, and got out to a ten-point lead. I remember thinking to myself, *Hey, this coaching thing is pretty easy!* Those thoughts, like our lead, didn't last.

It stayed close for most of the game, but their defense was tough. And that Carmelo kid turned out to become pretty good. We shot 1 of 11 on threes in the second half, and Melo put up 28 on us. When both our point guards fouled out with six minutes to go, we were done. We ended up losing by fifteen, but I still felt good about how we had played and our chances for the season. That Syracuse team, after all, ended up winning the national title that season.

Our next game, and my first win as a head coach, came against Indiana State. The Sycamores are probably most famous for having Larry Bird on their team and making the championship game in 1979. Well, Larry Bird was no longer on the team, and we beat them by twenty-five. One of the things I did differently than my dad was I changed up our offense a little bit. My dad loved the motion offense, where players are all moving and cutting based on how the defense is playing and what the person with the ball is doing. I preferred to run more set plays, where we had a clear plan on where to go and who would shoot. Early in the season, no one had seen our sets yet, so they were fairly effective. Early in the season, as we had success, I was excited. "See, we should have been running more sets!" Of course, as those plays get scouted, the defenses know what you are trying to do, and so they become less effective.

When you coach at a school like Valparaiso, you're really using your nonconference schedule to prepare you for the teams you'll play in conference. Because the only way you'll make the NCAA tournament is by winning that conference tournament—so everything becomes about getting the best seed and preparing for March. When we lost three straight road games to Cincinnati, Loyola (Chicago), and Milwaukee, I was just looking for improvement more than the results.

We had a big win against Central Michigan and Chris Kaman, who played in the NBA from 2003 to 2016, and that made me think we were turning a corner and heading in the right direction. But then, our first game after Christmas, we took the short bus ride to West Lafayette, Indiana, for our game at Purdue. Their coach, Gene Keady, is a legend in Indiana basketball, and the court was literally named after him when we played there. Like many teams before us that traveled to Mackey Arena, we got worked. Even worse? We got outworked. Losing by thirty-two isn't what bothered me. Yes, I was bothered that we lost by that much. But mostly I was bothered by the lack of effort from the team, specifically on defense. We weren't getting back after we put up a shot, and we weren't getting matched up with their players when they pushed the tempo. I hadn't seen that before from our guys, and I made sure they knew I didn't want to see it again. Some nights you won't make shots, but the one thing you can control on a basketball court is how much effort you give. Watching the film of the Purdue game with the team, we were all embarrassed by our energy and intensity. The next game, I made sure our effort would be better.

Normally, the day before a game, you don't really run sprints or have that hard of a practice. But for our next game after Purdue, we traveled to Missouri, and we made sure the players knew that our effort needed to improve. We ran them hard and demanded some accountability from the players. And the next day, instead of a shootaround before the game, we had loose ball drills and charge drills, where our players had to dive on the ground and take physical contact in order to keep their opponents from scoring. You don't normally do that, because players could get hurt, but I thought it was important. They needed to see, feel, and believe that, no matter what, this is how we're going to compete. This is how we're going to play.

We lost to Missouri by eighteen, but I saw a difference in our approach, and the game was actually a lot closer than the final score. One of the Missouri assistants after the game commented on how well coached we were. That meant a lot, but we had more work to do because our next game was in Chicago against Notre Dame.

Notre Dame was ranked No. 6 in the country and was like a big brother who always beat us up. South Bend was only fifteen minutes away, but as a Big East school with millions in resources, they were on another planet.

One of Colorado's old football coaches, Bill McCartney, who helped start the Promise Keepers ministry, wrote a book that has a lot of wisdom. One of McCartney's go-to motivational things was to meet with each player on the team. In the meeting, he'd look the player in his eyes and ask him, "What am I going to get from you today? What are you, as a man, going to provide?"

Sometimes the players say things like "I'm going to make my free throws." But this time I was looking for, and before that game I got, things like "I'm going to give everything I have." "I'm going to be the first to the floor for a loose ball." I wanted them to understand that Notre Dame might have better players, but they shouldn't have better effort.

That was the first time I'd ever done meetings like that before a game. And since, I've only maybe done it four or five other times. But that day, in an NBA arena in downtown Chicago, my guys stepped up. Their effort and intensity couldn't have been better. We looked like a team that was playing their hardest, that wanted to compete. And we competed. We were down two with ten seconds to go, and we got a wide-open three-pointer for Greg Tonagel, our senior point guard and team captain after he had stolen the ball and given us a chance to win. He missed and we lost by two.

As heartbreaking as the loss was, our fans were fired up. This is the team that we thought we would have this season. We knew we had found the right gear. Now we just had to stay there.

Our conference schedule started the next game, and we just started rolling. We went 12–2 in our conference that season, the best record we had ever had in school history up to that point, and good enough for the top seed going into the conference tournament. It was just like I had seen my dad do so many times. He won our conference regular season seven out of the last eight seasons, and won the conference tournament six times, so that's definitely what I was expecting. And if we won the conference tournament, we would go to the NCAA tournament, and we would have been a pick to score an upset over someone. My first year as a head coach was lining up in the best way possible.

But here's the thing: no matter how good of a regular season you've had, the three most stressful days in a mid-major coach's life are in the conference tournament, especially when you've won your conference and had a great season. At a mid-major, it really doesn't matter how you do in the regular season. If you win the conference tournament, you're in the NCAA tournament. If not, you're watching TV like everyone else. At a Power Five school, your postseason is made in January and February because that's when you're winning the games that will help you make the tournament. For coaches at big schools, I think there's more pressure over the ten weeks of your conference schedule. But for teams like Valpo, there is no more pressure than those three days of the conference tournament.

The tournament was held in Kemper Arena in Kansas City, so we didn't get home court advantage for winning the regular season. But we still started the tournament really strong. We beat Chicago State by twenty and then played University of Missouri–Kansas City in the semifinals. Now, with the tournament being held in Kansas City, and the fact that they were one of only two losses we had during conference play, I was concerned. But we played with the same effort we had shown all year and won by twenty-one, sending us to the conference championship and one game away from my first chance at One Shining Moment. We played Indiana University–Purdue University Indianapolis (IUPUI). And I thought Valparaiso was hard to say.

As difficult as their name was to pronounce, the game was even harder. We trailed for most of the game because we just couldn't hit any shots. Their coach, Ron Hunter, had their team ready to play. We had defeated IUPUI twice already that season, but both games were fairly close. And there's a saying in college basketball: the hardest thing to do is beat a team three times. It was proving to be true.

The game was close throughout, and we went to the last few seconds tied at 64. They gave the ball to Matt Crenshaw, their point guard who had served six years in the Navy, so he was like twenty-seven years old. One thing I didn't know then, but found out later, was that as part of his service, he served on a ship called the USS *Kansas City*. Unfortunately for us, in that city, he hit the shot that sank our season.

It was another quintessential March Madness moment, but this time I was on the losing end. Losing is never fun, but when you lose out on a chance to go to the NCAA tournament when someone else hits a shot at the buzzer, it's especially not fun.

That's the thing about trusting in God. In life, someone else's victory sometimes means your defeat. But God can use your defeat to strengthen you in ways a victory might not have accomplished. Is it always fun? Absolutely not. But you can trust that it's good.

> **God can use your defeat to strengthen you in ways a victory might not have accomplished.**

I remember in the arena hallway after the game, an article on our team and the job we had done in the first year was published by Dennis Dodd with CBS SportsLine. It was a weird moment of feeling like the work we did was recognized at one of our lowest moments of the season, so that made me feel a little bit better. But one thing I've always felt that God has given me is an ability to be positive. So even at the time when the one door I had been hoping to go through was closed, I got to work on opening other ones.

I got on the phone that night and started working to get us an invitation to the National Invitation Tournament, which is the tournament teams go to if they don't make the NCAA tournament. Some teams and coaches are disappointed to not make March Madness and have been known to turn down invitations to the NIT just because it can feel anticlimactic. But for our team, I saw it as an opportunity. And I let the NIT organizers know that we would go wherever they wanted if they invited us.

On Sunday night, the NCAA tournament bracket was announced, and then the NIT started to invite the teams that were left out. The NCAA games start on the Thursday after what's called Selection Sunday, so the NIT plays games on the Monday and Tuesday before that to try to get people to watch their games on TV. We knew we were going somewhere but didn't know where until the NIT had it all sorted out. On Sunday night we got the call and found out we would be playing Iowa, which was a four-hour bus ride away. So off we went, headed to Iowa City for a game that ended up being the only game on TV the next night. So, to me, even though I'd rather have been in the NCAA tournament, I still saw a lot of positives in the situation. We had a national television audience, which was great exposure for our team and our brand.

We ended up losing to Iowa by two, which officially ended our season and my first year as a head coach. After the game, having lost our last two games by two points each, there was some frustration about what might have been. But I felt like it was important to emphasize that it was a good moment and not a bad one.

The conference season was really good. Not going to the NCAA tournament hurt, of course, but we still got the experience of going to the NIT. We also had an excellent recruiting class coming in.

We had been very close in the Syracuse game, and the season had revealed them to be an incredibly talented team. We had a chance to beat Notre Dame, who ended up as a No. 5 seed in the NCAA tournament and would make the Sweet 16. The point is, we were good. And if we had beaten IUPUI, I think we had a chance to do some damage in the NCAA tournament. But that didn't happen and now our season was over.

At the time I was frustrated for our players because I believed in them and badly wanted them to have every opportunity. But also, as a coach who was starting my own career, I knew what happened if you won games in the NCAA tournament. When you are at a small school, if you make the tournament and win a game, you can be presented with other opportunities to coach at bigger schools that have a chance to win a national championship. Losing out on the tournament meant losing out on a chance to take the next step in my career. Or so I thought.

FIVE

CHASE THE FIRE

But Joseph said to them, "Don't be afraid. Am I in the place of God?"

GENESIS 50:19

One of my fondest memories of college basketball doesn't have anything to do with my being anywhere near a basketball court. Obviously I grew up around the game, watching my dad coach. But as I got older and started to understand the larger basketball universe and where we fit into it at Bethel College, I really grew to love the NCAA tournament. Specifically, I loved how at the end of the championship game, CBS would play the "One Shining Moment" song and show the best plays from the tournament. My favorite basketball memory is being in junior high, sitting in my living room in Mishawaka, Indiana, with my family and watching those highlights and listening to that song. It was like looking through a telescope into a different planet. My dad's school wasn't even eligible for the tournament, so they would never have a chance to make that video, but it was this exotic and aspirational place that we got to see each March. And I think at some point we got the "One Shining Moment" song on a cassette as a single, and we would sit around and listen to that over and over again. Like, no disrespect to "Endless Love," but that's definitely my favorite Luther Vandross song.

That's why losing in my first conference tournament as a head coach was so tough. As a first-year coach, I spent the season trying to be like my dad but at the same time trying to do my own thing because I believed in the principles and concepts they were based on. To lose to IUPUI the way we did, in the championship game, and have that be the way we missed a chance to have a shot at our own One Shining Moment was both devastating for me, in terms of how I felt for our players, but also motivating. That's the thing about losing. It's just a reminder of the opportunity you have to get better.

I started that off-season looking for ways to make our team better. We had a good recruiting class lined up that was ranked No. 1 in our conference and in the top 35 nationally, so I felt we had some momentum. And I was adding to our team in other ways too.

One of my assistants, Mike Heideman, who had just joined my staff the previous year, was taking a job as an assistant with Dick Bennett at Washington State. That meant I had an opening for a new assistant, and I was being told by administrators at Valpo that I needed to hire an older coach. Well, at thirty-eight, Matt Driscoll might not have been considered old by too many people. But compared to me, he became the veteran of our staff.

Coach Driscoll—or "Dris," as I call him—had been at Clemson for five years under Larry Shyatt. I had met him a few years before when I was an assistant coach, and he was one of the first people I thought of when I knew I'd need to make a new hire. A walking cup of coffee, Coach Driscoll is fast talking, fast thinking, and hardworking. And since he was the president of the Assistant Coaches Association, he had a lot of contacts.

One thing I'll never forget about Coach Driscoll, though, is when

I was interviewing him for the job, he asked me a question. He said, "Coach, your dad was here for a long time. Are you trying to be like your dad?"

Now, I had been a head coach for one season. And I'd just missed out on a chance to experience March Madness for the first time as a head coach because we lost in the finals of our conference tournament. At other schools, in bigger conferences, you can make the NCAA tournament without winning your conference because you get what are called "at-large" bids.

In some ways I was very much trying to be like my dad. I wanted to be a good family man; I wanted to be a good leader and godly example for the players and people in my life. But if the opportunity came, I also wanted to be at a place where it would be easier to make the tournament and win a national championship. I told Coach Driscoll that I loved Valpo. But my dream was still to win a title and experience that One Shining Moment.

If God has put something on your heart, don't think it's an accident. God is big enough for our dreams. In fact, he's the one who gave them to us in the first place. Since I was a child, I'd always wanted to be a part of March Madness. To have a "One Shining Moment" of my own.

The chance to chase my dream came way sooner than I was expecting.

Just a few weeks later, Coach Driscoll and I were in Los Angeles for a networking retreat. Coach Driscoll really thought we should go and make connections, plus it was a fundraiser for cancer treatment, and the guys who ran the retreat, brothers David and Dana Pump, were big in the California high school basketball scene. It made sense on a lot of levels. By this point, Baylor had been featured on the news for over a month. We knew that a player had been

If God has put something on your heart, don't think it's an accident.

murdered and that another player had confessed. Patrick Dennehy's memorial service had been held the night before the event we were attending in Los Angeles.

The keynote speaker that evening was legendary UCLA basketball coach John Wooden. Coach Driscoll and I sat at a table alongside Tim Floyd, the head coach of the NBA's New Orleans Hornets, where my brother, Bryce, was playing at the time. Hours earlier, Dave Bliss had resigned as head coach at Baylor. Given the amount of attention the Baylor scandal had received, his resignation made sense and made headline news. As soon as Coach Driscoll heard the news, he was in my ear. "Man, you'd be great for that job." Now, that was flattering to hear. But I was also Coach Driscoll's boss, and it never hurts to make your boss feel good about himself. But as we sat around the table, waiting for the legendary coach from UCLA to address us, the topic of the Baylor opening came up in our conversation. "Actually, you would be really great for that job," Tim Floyd said. "You're young; you're Christian; you're energetic."

Again, nice to hear, but I was a young guy with one year of head-coaching experience. I wasn't sure I could even get an interview, let alone the job. But then Coach Floyd said he knew the women's coach at Baylor. He pulled out his phone, called her, and said, "I need to get the president on the phone."

I couldn't believe it.

The next day we flew back to Indiana, but the idea that I might be a candidate for the Baylor job suddenly seemed very real. Coach Floyd was very optimistic I would get an interview, and once I was contacted by Bob Beaudine, the headhunter Baylor had hired to help with their search, I knew I was officially in the running. Suddenly, I had a choice to make. Did I want this job? Baylor had announced that it was self-imposing penalties, including probation, meaning it wouldn't be eligible for postseason play for the next season. My dream of having my One Shining Moment would be delayed at the least.

Did I really want to leave Valpo after one year? What did I really even know about what had happened in Waco? I did what I usually did when I had a decision to make. I prayed; talked to Kelly; and talked to my dad.

The thing my dad kept saying to me was, first, with God, anything can happen. Philippians tells us quite clearly that with Christ, all things are possible. And I had never seen anyone, be it my dad, my brother, or me, go wrong by betting on God. So that part wasn't really tough at all. And then my dad also reminded me that anything I did there would be an improvement. Baylor could only move upward—there was nowhere to go lower than where they were. So while some people saw it as a job filled with obstacles, some potentially unconquerable, after praying about it, I felt led to go to Baylor.

It was a head coach position in a major conference and a faith-based school. If things worked out, I would be able to live out my faith and to have a chance to get to the Final Four. I told Mr. Beaudine I would take the interview, and he arranged for me to meet him; the president of the university, Dr. Robert Sloan; David Brooks, the school's CFO; and Jim Turner, a board member at the school and a former player who was heading up the search, at a Chicago airport conference room in a couple of days.

Once I knew I was getting the interview, I was all in. I wanted to make sure they got to know me, my passion for coaching, and my passion for connecting. So I did what I had been doing my entire coaching career—I started recruiting.

I wanted to cast a vision not for what the job was at the moment but what it could be. The people at Baylor needed to see how, in the midst of their brokenness, their redemption could reflect God's glory.

From the outside, it was easier for me to see what was possible rather than what was. That's what I was selling them.

I had Coach Driscoll make up fake *USA Today* front pages with headlines that read, "Baylor Goes from Probation to the Final Four!" The newspaper copies even had made-up stories to go with it, including names of recruits we would get from Texas. Armed with those and my binders of stats and selling points I used with actual recruits, my dad and I drove up to Chicago. We got into the room where the interview would be held a few hours early and started decorating.

Now, the idea of two grown men decorating a conference room with green and gold streamers may seem a little silly. But that's exactly what my dad and I did. We literally covered the room in Baylor Green and Gold. And since I knew that Jim Turner, who was heading up the search committee, was the CEO of Dr Pepper, I made sure we had lots of Dr Pepper in the room for everyone to drink. I've long believed that everyone wants to be recruited, so I was excited to show them what it felt like to have someone pursuing them. Even if I didn't get the job, being able to love people in times when they need it the most does as much for the person doing the loving as the person, or people, being loved.

With the room decorated, my dad left, and I sat there, alone in a green-and-gold conference room, ready to start the next chapter in my journey.

When the Baylor team arrived, their faces showed how surprised and excited they were to see the effort we had put into the room. Jim Turner later told me it was like walking into a birthday party for himself.

We sat down and I started selling. I let them know I was coming from Valparaiso, the largest Lutheran school in America. While I was there, I had learned the value of recruiting to your niche. I knew that if a player I was recruiting came from a Lutheran home, I at least had his mother or grandmother on my side. My belief, I told them, was that we could do the same at Baylor. I believed we could find players who both loved the game and who would appreciate a faith environment. Given what had happened recently, it definitely seemed like that component had been missing. I also shared with them that I had developed connections into some international recruiting circles that could prove extremely useful in a rebuild. Many overseas big men were looking for an offer to play against the best competition in the United States, and at Baylor we could offer that.

To their credit, the selection committee met my optimism with their reality. They talked about how much heavy lifting would be involved. They said they didn't know how many players I would have because Baylor and the NCAA had given every player on the team the ability to transfer to a different school without having to sit out a year. They also shared some of the details of the current situation that hadn't been in the news yet, about Coach Bliss and his involvement in some payments and some of the cover-up involved. They said because of that, and the evolving nature of the ongoing NCAA investigation, they couldn't say for certain how many scholarships would be taken away or how many years of probation they could get. They also asked me about my ability to handle a job like that at my age, since I was only thirty-two at the time, and with my relative lack of head-coaching experience.

It was a very long, honest conversation. They shared hard truths and asked difficult questions. But those types of exchanges tend to produce the best fruit.

I thought the whole interview went really well, and I felt good about my chances of getting the job, but before I left I had to tell them about my one condition. It was August, and I had a team I was responsible for getting ready to start practicing in a few weeks. I didn't feel right, as· excited as I was about the Baylor job, leaving my players, or the school, in a position to not have a head coach that soon before the season began. So I told them that my one condition, if they offered me the job, was that I was going to ask my dad if he would come out of retirement to coach our team at Valpo.

As a guy with so little head-coaching experience, I knew I wasn't exactly in a position to be making demands. But I felt strongly about it.

After a four-hour interview, the Baylor selection team boarded their private jet to travel on to the next candidate's interview. I got back in the car with my dad and returned to Valparaiso.

I'd like to say that I got the job because of my performance in that interview. And, to an extent, that might be true. I did find out that they admired my energy, my honest discussion about my faith, and how comfortable I was working in a Christian environment, and my optimism for what God could do at that school was refreshing. I guess they also liked the decorations. But honestly, part of why they offered me the job is that I actually wanted it.

After the interview, I found out they spoke to coaches at Air Force, the University of Missouri–Kansas City, and a few others. But a decent number of coaches just weren't interested. The reality was, Baylor hadn't been a coveted position even before the scandal. Before hiring Dave Bliss, Jim Turner had called Bill Self, who was coaching Tulsa at the time, to gauge his interest in the job. "No, thanks," Self told Turner. "I'm waiting for a *good* job." He ended up at Illinois, and then at Kansas, so I guess Bill knew what he was doing.

The Baylor team also reached out to Duke to see if they could get Mike Brey or another assistant, and I guess those calls didn't last very long.

I also know that they were comforted by the fact that they knew my dad. Jim Turner actually knew him from when my dad's Valparaiso teams played in the Dr Pepper Invitational in Waco, and Jim was their tournament liaison. I'm sure knowing my family and their values helped. And, as I said earlier, there's no question that the exposure the Drew name and Valparaiso brand got when Bryce hit "The Shot" made other people more comfortable with me. I was definitely the least well-known of the three Drew men. And I couldn't have been more grateful for the other two!

Again, the roots of God's plan for us are woven throughout the soil of our lives. Think about where God wants you to grow.

After a few days, Baylor called and offered me the job. Per our discussion, I made sure my father was comfortable coming out of retirement and taking over at Valparaiso and that Valparaiso was good too. It is amazing how God works things out, because after sitting out a year, my dad was rejuvenated and had missed coaching. So this turned out to be a blessing for him to coach again at Valpo. And I also made sure to have a clause inserted into my contract that would get me an extra year for each year of probation that the NCAA added, if that was going to happen.

> **The roots of God's plan for us are woven throughout the soil of our lives.**

I accepted the job. Without visiting the campus. Seriously—imagine taking a job without ever visiting the place you're going to call home! I also accepted without talking to anyone else who was familiar with the situation. The salary wasn't really that much of an improvement from my Valparaiso salary, but that wasn't the point. It was an opportunity to pursue my dream, and I didn't have much time to waste. Three of Baylor's best players, John Lucas, Kenny Taylor, and Lawrence Roberts, had announced they were transferring to other schools and would be leaving Waco's campus soon. Ever the optimist, I wanted to get down there and get in front of them and try to convince them to stay. If I was successful, we could have a decent team with some real talent on the roster.

I flew down with Coach Driscoll, Coach Morefield, and Kelly, on the Baylor plane. Coach Driscoll, who had just moved with his family to Indiana seven weeks before, was now moving to Waco to be on my staff. As we were boarding the plane I noticed he was getting on with way more stuff than you would normally take on an airplane, let alone a small one like this.

"Dris, what are you doing?" I asked him.

"Coach, I'm not coming back here. This is everything I have. Once we get to Waco, I'm going to work and staying there."

Well, the pilots told him that there wasn't enough room in the storage area for his stuff and the only way we could fit all of his things on the plane was to put them in the restroom.

"Then put it in the restroom," he said matter-of-factly.

What Coach Dris didn't know was that Kelly was actually pregnant with our first child. It was going to be a long two-hour flight for Kelly but never the one to complain, she rode it out and made it to Waco, no problem. I still like to tease Coach Driscoll that my pregnant wife couldn't use the restroom so he would have a place to hang his sports coats.

The next day, we had the press conference scheduled in the morning, which we had worked out to be at the same time in Waco for me as the one they were having back in Indiana for my dad. I knew my dad would be fine, but some Baylor people weren't so sure about me. They made us take media training for several hours the night before, making sure we knew how to address the situation in Waco with the gravity and authenticity it deserved. I might struggle to be as serious as I should be sometimes, but I pride myself on being authentic.

The next day, I walked up to the microphone and declared that our goal was to win a national title. My claim generated some headlines the next day. But God was the One who was writing the ultimate story.

SIX

GATHER STONES

"Ask and it will be given to you; seek and you will find; knock and the door will be opened to you."

MATTHEW 7:7

I'd like to say that I remember a lot of things about when we first set foot on the Baylor campus and that I made sure to take it all in as we got the tour of the area before the press conference the next day. But that isn't true for several reasons. First, my memory is not that great. That's what made Coach Driscoll a good partner. Even today, he'll be like, "The press conference was on August 22, 2003. That was a Friday. And it was about ninety-two degrees." I don't really have any clue what day of the week it was, but I do remember that it was hot. August in Texas feels different from August in Indiana.

I also remember when we walked into the office, one of the things Coach Driscoll pointed out was the sign in front of the arena that said Men's Basketball Office. That sign had been the one you saw on all the networks in any of their coverage of Patrick Dennehy's absence and the ensuing scandal. We'd walk by that sign almost every day, not that we needed much reminding of the job we had inherited.

We got to work trying to change the culture and lay the foundation for what we wanted to build even before the press conference. And I'm proud to say, among the most important things we did was my mom's idea. Our first gathering when we were in the office was simple: we prayed. Me, the coaches, Kelly, Bryce, my mom, and a few others held hands in a circle and asked God that his glory would be seen in that office and in our efforts at Baylor.

Too often we can see the work to be done and forget about the role God can and should play in it. When you have what seems like an impossible task, don't forget to ask Jesus to make the impossible possible and seek his guidance throughout.

> **When you have what seems like an impossible task, don't forget to ask Jesus to make the impossible possible.**

There were three key players who had announced they were transferring to other schools, and I was hoping to change their minds, and I was thinking that would be a cool way for God to help answer that particular prayer. He had other plans, I guess.

The players who hadn't announced they were transferring were all hanging around the office when I got there. I was excited to meet them but also tried to be sensitive to what they were going through. Our staff was walking into a new job that, despite the circumstances, represented a big chance for us, our families, and our careers. These guys just had a teammate murdered and another teammate confess to the crime. Then they lost the head coach who recruited them and had to read about the new allegations and revelations in the news or see it on TV every day. And all of this came while trying to make decisions about their own futures, in and outside of basketball. In basketball, what looked like it would have been a talented team with a chance to make the NCAA tournament for the first time in their lifetime had just turned into a situation where the team not only wouldn't be good; they wouldn't even have the chance to compete in the Big 12 tournament as a result of Baylor's self-imposed punishment. And there was always the chance of additional NCAA sanctions. Outside of basketball, the players had gone from being local celebrities to local outcasts. Whereas they were once celebrated for being the best examples of how walking in faith can lead you to new heights, they now were known for being a part of the team that was in the deepest of holes.

We walked into all of that. Looking back, we probably should have prayed in that office a little longer.

As much as anything else, I thought it was important that we convince the remaining eight that we wanted them. Not only did we want them, we wanted them to be a part of the successful program we planned on building. Now, I might be pretty naive and overly optimistic a lot of the times, but I try not to be a total idiot. I knew this would be a tough sell. I may have been a relatively inexperienced head coach, but I had come from a program that won conference championships at Valpo. We met with the players individually, and we showed them the ring box of the rings we'd won previously at Valpo. Now, that may seem silly. But when you play sports competitively, you like to win. And in college basketball you like to win championships. When you win championships, you get rings.

This was tough. Based on Baylor's penalties, we knew we couldn't win a conference championship that season, even if we had the kind of team that could realistically compete for one. And to be honest, even though the players were still on the team, they weren't necessarily thrilled to be there. One of the returning seniors on the team, guard Matt Sayman, would write a book about his experience at Baylor before, during, and after the scandal. In the book he writes about how, when he found out Dave Bliss was resigning, he called around to see if he could transfer. What he admits is, as a player with only one year of eligibility, he didn't have any other options. So as coaches, we were having to confront not only a depleted roster because of the players who had left but also a depleted spirit in some of the ones who remained. That's where the ring boxes came in. We were selling them on the idea that, while they might not be able to win a ring this year, they could establish a culture and a foundation for a program that *could* win a championship.

I took it as a good sign when all the players came to the press conference. That's why I made it a point to say there were players there who would make fans proud.

And I really was grateful for the eight who stayed. In life, I think God uses our process as much as our progress. We are shaped by the experiences God has for us, and I think that shaping equips us for the next parts of our journeys.

> **We are shaped by the experiences God has for us, and I think that shaping equips us for the next parts of our journeys.**

At the same time, I knew we needed more players. As soon as the press conference was over, Coach Dris and I got to work on trying to get in front of the players who had been at Baylor and announced they were leaving. In fact, we had almost started the night before.

Lawrence Roberts was six foot nine, had made the All-Big 12 freshman team, and was clearly the team's best player as a sophomore. He had also just announced he was going to transfer to Mississippi State. Now, we had been trying to get on the phone with him and his family while we were still in Indiana, just to see if we could get in front of him. Once we landed in Waco, Coach Dris and I almost rented a car and drove overnight to where he was, with the plan of trying to see him for a little bit before he left for Starkville and so we could get back in time for the press conference. I remember Marilyn Crone was riding with us, listening in and saying, "You guys are crazy if you think you're gonna drive all night, talk to a player, then drive back in time for the press conference."

She wasn't wrong.

It's like in *Top Gun* when Iceman says Maverick is dangerous. We were crazy. But we'd also been effective. I might not have had much of a name nationally, but I did have a reputation and a track record of being a good recruiter. I'd been named recruiter of the year by a recruiting service while an assistant coach at Valpo—a recognition that people at smaller schools didn't typically get. I was confident that if we got in front of somebody, we had a chance of signing him up.

ESPN star Robin Roberts was Lawrence Roberts's aunt. We had a relationship with Robin from an ESPY event after Bryce's shot, and we were able to get him on the phone. The bad news: he was locked into going to Mississippi State. The good news was we didn't have to drive all night. If you ever see the video of the press conference and I seem well rested, that's why.

We had similarly bad luck with the other star players from the previous season. John Lucas III was an incredibly quick, talented point guard. His dad, John Lucas Jr., was an NBA legend and had coached in the NBA for several different teams. There was some talk that he would be a candidate for the Baylor job. I knew him from some NBA connections, and he was great about giving us a chance to talk to his son. Unfortunately, John Lucas III decided to transfer to Oklahoma State, which at the time was an incredibly strong program. They'd beaten Baylor by fifty the season before. Losing John to the Cowboys didn't make me more confident about our prospects when we headed up there this season. Lastly, Kenny Taylor was the team's best shooter the season before. Despite our best efforts, he decided to transfer as well. And like John, he was going to another Big 12 school: Texas. I never begrudged anyone's decision to go and pursue a chance to play on a team that would be eligible for postseason play and a chance at a championship. (After all, I came to Baylor to pursue that One Shining Moment.) But it didn't mean I was excited about it.

Knowing we would have to begin the season with so few scholarship players, Coach Driscoll and I turned our focus inward. We needed to find bodies.

As coaches, we were always watching the film and traveling to high school tournaments to try to see as many potential recruits as possible. But that fall, we did a lot of scouting on our own campus. We literally would just walk around and stop anyone who looked athletic and was taller than six foot three.

It got sort of comical. One of us or an assistant might be walking down a sidewalk on one side of the green, see a six-foot-four person coming the other way, and would find a way to end up walking with him for a while. And it wasn't just on campus.

One night, after a long day in the office, Coach Driscoll and I went out for a quick dinner at the local Fazoli's. We were in the drive-through, probably asking for extra breadsticks, when we spotted a young man inside the restaurant who had to be six foot seven. Suddenly, I didn't care about dinner. I kind of swerved over to the side and Coach Driscoll jumped out, meeting the guy as he was walking out of the restaurant.

Now, I don't know how awkward you might think an interaction would be between a tall kid we've never met before leaving a Fazoli's and Coach Driscoll peppering him with questions about where he goes to school, whether he's ever played basketball, and how much free time he has. But I can tell you this conversation was at least that awkward. Turns out, he played music, not sports, and wasn't really interested in taking up any new hobbies. Never one to take rejection easily, we kept an eye out for him on campus for the next few weeks, hoping to get another chance to change his mind.

We also tried more conventional ways of attracting walk-on talent: we held a tryout. To advertise the tryout, we sent out a release on our website and in the local media on October 6. It was pretty straight-forward. It began, "The Baylor men's basketball coaching staff has scheduled walk-on tryouts for Oct. 20 at the Ferrell Center. Students wishing to participate in the tryout must complete the following steps to be eligible to participate on Oct. 20."

The first bullet point said, "Must be a currently enrolled Baylor student."

Well, the tryout started, and Coach Driscoll walked in, and the gym was buzzing, both with people on the court to try out and people in the stands to watch. It was our first public event we were doing as a new staff, and it was nice to see some energy and positivity on the Baylor court. I looked around and thought to myself, *Man, this is excit-ing. Look at all these people who want to come join us. This is going to be great news for the school. God is going to use this to make some really good things come out of what's transpired.* That's what I was thinking. Coach Driscoll saw one guy, probably six foot eight, putting up some shots with a nice, smooth shooting stroke and walked over to him.

Seeing them talking, I convinced myself that this kid could start, and maybe we would win more games than I thought. There were a few other guys in the gym who looked like him. Now, Coach Driscoll has this thing called the two-second rule. You need to wait two seconds after someone has stopped talking to see if they're done or if they have any additional information they're trying to relay. So, Coach asked him what year he was in. And the young man replied that he was a sophomore.

"Sophomore, huh?" Coach Driscoll said, the excitement and our projected win totals rising with every syllable. "What's your major?"

"Yes, I'm a sophomore—at McLennan Community College."

Sometimes I hate the two-second rule.

As soon as he said he went to McLennan, the community college in Waco, I knew we had a problem. So did Coach Driscoll. And the problem would only get worse.

"Oh, awesome," Coach Driscoll replied. "So are you here by yourself, or do you have some teammates and friends with you?"

When he said his teammates were there as well, Coach Driscoll went into crisis mode. He has this ability to whistle very loudly, and he used it very effectively in that moment. He got everyone's attention and asked the crowd to split up, with the people who go to Baylor on one court and the people who don't on the other. Almost all of the tall people ended up on the "We don't go to Baylor" court.

Sometimes as a coach, you have to do tough things. And that day, Coach Driscoll did one of them. He told the people on the non-student court that there had been an incredible miscommunication. We were so sorry, but they wouldn't be able to try out or be on the team. For some reason, even though the release we put out was pretty explicit, something got lost in translation, and lots of people showed up thinking it was open to anyone. We found out later that one family had come from out of town, like Dallas or Houston, actually got into an accident on the way to the tryout, and still found a way to get there, only to be told they wouldn't be eligible to play.

For the ones who could play, there wasn't much left. We ended up with one player. Robbie McKenzie was six foot five and an athletic kid who had played basketball in high school. More importantly, he was a Baylor student. He came to Baylor to study medicine and would go on to become a doctor. I'm forever thankful for the triage he helped us with throughout that season. Robbie joined Will Allen, Turner Phipps, Ryan Prior, and Nino Etienne as walk-ons who were vital to our team that year.

Going into that fall, we thought we might be able to get some football players to help us out too. We did get one, Joe Simmons, a six-foot-five, 250-pound defensive end, for five games that year. But otherwise, it was the seven scholarship players who stayed and the few walk-ons, including Robbie, that we would have for our first year in a major conference.

I knew it was going to be a challenge. At least, I thought I did. We weren't playing for rings. We were laying the foundation. But I didn't realize how tough of a job we were all in for in year one.

SEVEN

ESTABLISH CULTURE

"For even the Son of Man did not come to be served, but to serve, and to give his life as a ransom for many."

MARK 10:45

New seasons mean new rhythms. But new rhythms don't have to mean new routines or habits. If we were going to be successful, I had to make sure that some of our older habits, specifically regular prayer and pursuit of intentional community, would continue, even as that first season at Baylor was so different.

First, I was starting a new job in a new city with a new team and new players, preparing for new opponents. Even though I had only been the head coach at Valpo for one season, I had been an assistant there for a decade, so there was a rhythm to the schedule and familiarity with the teams you played in conference each year. Now we had an entirely new schedule to scout and scheme, plus new players to try to identify and start the process of recruiting, new area coaches to meet and figure out how in the world we were going to prepare for Big 12 play with eight scholarship players. All of this to say, we were busy.

Things were different for me at work. They were also different for me at home. Kelly was newly pregnant. But that didn't stop her from taking on the task of moving us from Indiana pretty much by herself. One of the reasons I have a hard time using the first person is because at every step of my journey, God has placed people in my life to help me do the things he has for me. When I was younger, it was my mom, dad, brother, and sister. As an older coach, my assistants and staff have been invaluable. And as a new coach in Waco who had a to-do list longer than the list of scholarship players at my disposal, having Kelly by my side, even figuratively, made the biggest difference in the world.

Kelly had gone back to Indiana after I accepted the job and, after a couple of months, moved most of our stuff down to Texas in a U-Haul. We lived in an off-campus apartment while our Waco home was under construction. As our season progressed, so did her pregnancy. But she still made another trip back to Indiana and packed up the rest of our lives in January while working to sell our house there. By March our home was ready, and Kelly moved us into our house just two weeks before giving birth to our daughter.

Between her pregnancy, moving across the country, and supporting all that we were trying to build at Baylor, I definitely don't think her life got any easier as she made the move south.

Neither, for the record, did mine.

While waiting for Kelly to move to Waco, I was living with Coach Driscoll in what was essentially student housing. I had lived with my parents when I first started my coaching career at Valpo, so I wasn't exactly high-maintenance as a roommate. Which is good, because our little apartment wasn't exactly high-end living. That actually was perfect, because it ensured we didn't want to be there much. One thing about Coach Driscoll, me, and the rest of the staff we had in place: we weren't afraid of work. In the beginning, that's all we did. We'd be grinding all day until 1:00 or 2:00 a.m., go home, sleep a few hours, then wake up and do it again. It was like *Groundhog Day*, except I didn't have Sonny and Cher waking me up every morning. I had walking-caffeine-drip Coach Driscoll. I had never been a big coffee guy before, but Coach Driscoll eventually ended up getting me hooked on freshly roasted beans!

One of the things on the top of my list was implementing the foundation of what we wanted to become as a program. I had shown the players the ring boxes because I wanted them to think about what it would look like to play for championships and, more importantly, the kind of mindset and work ethic it would require. But we also had to lay a spiritual foundation. Luckily, once again God put the right person in my life.

He has a habit of doing that—putting the right people in our lives. It's up to us to be open to letting them in so they can make the impact God sent them to make.

One day I was in the office and a man walked in and introduced himself to me as Mark Wible, the associate pastor of a local church, and he told me that he was the chaplain for the team. *Awesome!* I thought. And I started giving him some of my ideas and expectations for what the spiritual component of our team's workouts would look like. I wanted them to hold chapel services before our games, and I told Pastor Wible it'd be great if he could deliver a message for about fifteen minutes each home game.

Well, what I found out later was that Pastor Wible was the team chaplain in a looser sense of the word. He had coached at Richfield High School in Waco and, between that and his role with Highland Baptist in town, he had been around and had become the chaplain by default.

I was looking for more, and not just because of everything that had happened before. Pastor Wible now had a more formal and demanding role. He told me later that it was kind of like a moment when the dog is chasing the 18-wheeler, only this time he actually caught it. He had never led a team's chapel services or been formally in charge of leading them spiritually, and he didn't really know what to do. Plus, Baptist preachers in Waco, Texas, aren't really used to delivering a message in the fifteen minutes I was asking.

But, like always, God provided.

The main interstate in Waco is I-35, which runs north to south. It runs from Mexico to Minnesota, but if you're going to Dallas or Austin or San Antonio, you're taking I-35. Well, there used to be a church on the side of I-35 that touted that they had a thirty-minute worship service with a fifteen-minute sermon. There are a lot worse things advertised on interstates than that, right?

So Pastor Wible called and asked about it, and they told him that they did indeed do a whole church sermon in only fifteen minutes. And so he told me, "Hey, if they can do it in a church, I guess I can do it in fifteen minutes. After all, we don't take up an offering."

Like Pastor Wible, we were making do with what we had.

While he was game-planning for how to instruct spiritually, Coach Driscoll, Coach Tang, and the rest of our staff tried to figure out how in the world we could be competitive with only eight scholarship players. Generally speaking, we knew we weren't going to have the most talent or even the most athleticism since we would be relying on walk-on players. As coaches, we had to figure out how to engineer a strategy that made the most of what we had while not expending all our players' energy. Our bench was going to be short, so playing high energy—run up and down the court on offense and then play super aggressive defense—wouldn't have worked. Or, at least, it wouldn't have worked for very long.

We decided to slow the game down. We installed an offense that called for the players to passively pass the ball around the perimeter for the first twenty seconds of the shot clock, while our other players ran around on the baseline and elbow and set screens for one another.

It was basically a way to make it look like we were running an offense, while in reality we were holding the ball. Dean Smith, the legendary North Carolina coach, made an offense based on similar principles famous with the "four corners" offense, where players took turns holding the ball in the four corners of the court for long stretches at a time. Of course, by 2003 we had a thirty-five-second shot clock, so that wasn't allowed anymore. Also, I'm nowhere near as good a coach as Dean Smith. We called our offense, appropriately, "false motion."

On defense we ran a zone defense, where the players have an area of the court they are responsible for and they don't have to chase the players on the other team around. Both concepts were designed to save the players' energy.

We also set parameters for how players should act on and off the court.

One of the problems the team had in previous years was with substance abuse. Faking drug test results or just not issuing the tests were among the allegations the NCAA was investigating. We let the players know that there would be no tolerance for using illegal drugs. But we wanted to go deeper than that. We also told them no profanity at practice or in games, and any violations would be met with push-ups as punishment. As a staff, we held ourselves to the same standard.

Some of the players thought we were kidding. But we wanted to instill a culture of discipline and loving respect, and we felt like taking that step was important. We were told it was a fairly dramatic departure from the previous regime.

A month after we held that walk-on tryout, our season was beginning. We had set a goal of winning fifteen games that season, one more than the team had won the year prior. Before the game, Pastor Wible talked to us about—what else?—David and Goliath. He told us how David only had a slingshot and a rock, with no sword or armor, but, with God's help, that was all he needed. David's aim was true, and after

Goliath fell, David went to the fallen giant, took out Goliath's sword, and cut off his head, holding it up so that all could see what God could make possible.

For a first-timer, Pastor Wible had nailed it. Which was good, because we were definitely going to need God's help. Before the first game we held a moment of silence to honor the memory of Patrick Dennehy, and we each wore a black strip on our jersey in his honor. Then our eight scholarship players and band of walk-ons went out and won the game, beating Texas Southern by thirteen. The win was a nice validation for the work and effort the team had put in. But the next few games brought us down to earth. We lost to teams like Stephen F. Austin and North Texas, smaller Texas schools that a Big 12 team should typically beat. If we were having a tough time with those teams, what would happen when we started playing teams in our conference?

Before we got that answer, we received more bad news.

Already low in numbers, we found out before our game against Louisiana–Monroe that one of our starters, Ellis Kidd, had violated team rules and had to be released from the team. This was devastating on a number of levels. First, our heart broke for Ellis, because you want to do all you can to help. Secondly, he was one of our eight scholarship players, so now a depleted squad was going to get even smaller.

The locker room was not a fun place to be when we broke the news to the team. They were shocked, sad, mad, and lots of other things. But I told them that as hard as it might be, there's a right way to do things. And that's what we were going to do. We had this one opportunity to do things the right way. And I told the remaining players that if they were going to be a part of this program, that's what we expected of them.

As sad as they were, our players responded the right way. We were down another player that game, so we only had six scholarship guys available. And Louisiana–Monroe hit a shot at the buzzer to force a second overtime, but our guys showed fight and resolve, and we won by six points, with four of our players playing more than forty minutes.

That win meant a lot to us as a staff because it made us feel like the players had our backs, holding the line when it came to how we wanted to do things. We knew it could cost us games. We knew we were replacing Ellis with a walk-on. But we weren't going to just look the other way. We had one chance to build this thing the right way, no matter what challenges we might face.

And trust me: there were challenges.

I'm famous for having a bad memory, or what Coach Driscoll calls a "selective memory." But there are a few things I will never forget about that first year in Waco.

First, while the losses were mounting, my faith was deepening. My dad, who was back in charge at Valpo, would call me and would read through the book of Job with me.

The Old Testament part of the Bible is broken up into books of history, books of poetry, and books of prophecy. Job, despite it being a story about a man who loses his family, livelihood, and friends to tragedy and then struggles with God over the reasons why, is considered a book of poetry.

> **We had one chance to build this thing the right way, no matter what challenges we might face.**

That the story of a man struggling to deal with the things God has put in his life, and his open questioning of God in that process, can be considered poetic is pretty awesome. That's real life. God is good. So is the struggle he gives us. And reading through Job with my dad helped remind me of that. Because there were a lot of struggles.

Entering Big 12 play, we were 5–8 and had just lost our last home game to Texas Rio Grande Valley. We lost our first three conference games by an average of twenty points. But we didn't get down. We were getting more consistent effort from our starters, and our five walk-ons had developed something of a cult following for their hustle and effort. When we put all five of them in the game at the same time (a move that earned them the nickname "The Hit Squad"), the crowd would offer some of the loudest applause of the game. In some ways, we were hitting our stride.

So, for that matter, was Pastor Wible. He was getting the hang of these fifteen-minute pregame services.

In the book of Matthew, Jesus was talking to his disciples about their frustration about not being able to drive out demons from a boy. And Jesus told them, "If you have faith as small as a mustard seed, you can say to this mountain, 'Move from here to there,' and it will move. Nothing will be impossible for you" (17:20).

And Pastor Wible had spent the past few chapels talking about having mustard seeds of faith and what could be possible. Before our home game against Iowa State, he brought in a visual aid to drive home the point. He went to the grocery store and bought a bottle of mustard seeds. And before the Iowa State game, he passed them around as part of his sermon and said, if you wanted the seed to take root, you'd have to ingest it. So here we were, all eating mustard seeds. Well, it happened that we won that game, our first Big 12 win of the season. And the two things that happened after that game that I remember were coming into the locker room and ceremoniously writing a big "1" on the white board for our first conference win, and all the players shouting about having a mustard-seed faith. After that, "a mustard seed of faith" became the theme for our chapels. How can you build on a mustard seed? What does it mean to grow in faith?

As our faith grew, so did our bond. While we lost our next few conference games, we were much more competitive, keeping the score close until our lack of depth caught up to us. When Texas A&M came to town, we felt like we had a chance. And we were right. Our effort throughout the season had begun to win over the fans, and we had more than seven thousand people watch us play our rivals from College Station. We got off to a fast start and won by what for us was a blowout: eight points. Our players went wild when I erased the "1" I had on the whiteboard and replaced it with a "2." Two conference wins through our first eight games. For most programs, that would be the sign of a losing season. For us, it was proof God was moving mountains.

But God was moving in other ways too. Our last win of the season came three weeks later, also against Texas A&M, but this time on the road. The game went into overtime, where our guys, who had faced adversity all season, took over. We won by six. But the thing I remember most from that game, the sign that what we were trying to instill was taking root, came in the postgame locker room. While Coach Tang and Coach Driscoll walked off the court with their arms around an exhausted Matt Sayman, the team was celebrating like we had done something much bigger than beat a team ranked lower than us. Our players shook sodas and water bottles and sprayed each other in the locker room, and then Terrance Thomas, one of the team's best players, erased the "2" we had on the board and replaced it with a "3."

The team went nuts, and I was so happy, not because of the win but because a player, a senior, had started to do the thing the coaches were demonstrating. He wrote the "3." He led the celebration. It was starting to become a player-led team. That's the kind of culture we wanted to build.

The last game of our season was at Oklahoma, a team that was ranked earlier in the year and that had beaten us by double digits at home.

Before the game I told our guys the game plan and the imperative that we wanted to make sure our physicality would be felt. This was our last game, so no sense in leaving anything in the tank. As I worked through my pregame speech, I got increasingly fired up. "We are going to keep their asses off the boards!" I told them. "And I will do push-ups for that."

The players loved it. And while I felt a little bad about it, I thought of the time I'd been spending reading the Bible with my dad. Job had lots of things to be frustrated about, and he wasn't shy about letting God hear about it.

We lost a close game in Norman that night, and in the locker room there were lots of tears, but also relief. As coaches, we went to each player and hugged him, and thanked him for what he'd done for the team that season as well as for the program's future. As a staff, we knew how hard the season had been. Despite an 8–21 record, we were proud of the work we had done, but more important was the buy-in the players had displayed. If we could keep getting that, and slowly improve the number and ability of players on the team, we felt like we had a clear plan for how we could move forward as a program.

God, as always, had other ideas.

EIGHT

SEEK GOD, NO MATTER THE SCORE

*Those who hope in the LORD will renew their strength.
They will soar on wings like eagles; they will run and not
grow weary, they will walk and not be faint.*

ISAIAH 40:31

In the world of college basketball, there's probably no one more respected or accomplished than Duke coach Mike Krzyzewski. He's won five national championships, been to a dozen Final Fours, coached the U.S. Olympic team to three gold medals, and has the most wins in college basketball history. But after his first few years, not too many people thought it would turn out that way. Coach K had losing seasons in his second and third years, and back then, there were lots of people who wanted to fire him.

That's probably the one thing I have in common with Coach K: our records weren't very good in our first few seasons.

I'd like to say that our team only got better after that first season and that it was a slow and steady, God-honoring rise that was nothing but a straight line moving upward. But God doesn't really work like that. At least he didn't at Baylor. If life is a roller-coaster ride, ours had more dips to endure.

The reality is, our team's record wasn't any better the following season. We lost some of the scholarship seniors we'd been able to rely on as part of what some referred to as the first season, and the players we were able to bring in were all young. So while we actually won one more game, going 9–21 on the year, we only won one Big 12 game. After beating Colorado in our third Big 12 game of the season, we lost the rest, ending the year on a fourteen-game losing streak.

We had some dips. Not that there weren't some positives.

We won a game at Purdue, which was amazing since we got blown out when I was at Valpo. The circumstances this time were equally as memorable. We went into the game with only six scholarship players, including a freshman guard, Aaron Bruce, who led the nation in freshman scoring that year. Now, that sounds impressive. And Aaron was good. He had led the Australian junior team to a gold medal in a world championship competition the summer before he came to the United States to play for us. But when you have limited scholarship players, players get to shoot the ball more than they might on a different team. And Aaron was a good shooter. We had several good shooters on that team. And that night at Purdue, we were making shots. With less than ten seconds left, we were up by three.

It's never easy to win on the road, especially at a place like Purdue. Coach Gene Keady is a legend for a reason, and they responded. They hit a three-pointer to tie the game with four seconds left. But not everyone realized the game was tied. One of their players thought they were still down one and fouled Aaron as soon as we got it in bounds. I was sort of shocked, but we had lost our previous road game by about forty at SMU, so we weren't complaining.

The crowd at Purdue was going crazy, and Aaron, even for someone who had won at the highest levels of international play, was still just a freshman. He missed the first free throw, which made the crowd even crazier. To his credit, he made the second, and we held on to win. It was a major moment for us as a program, to have the players we recruited step up in big-time situations and help us get a signature win. We really enjoyed ourselves in the visiting locker room afterward.

We didn't have too many moments to enjoy the rest of the season.

But I think God was in that too. Just like my first year at Baylor, my dad and I spent, at his suggestion, a lot of time reading through the book of Job that second season as well. At one point I said, "Dad, are there any other books of the Bible?" Which served as evidence that we needed to still be reading Job.

As frustrating as the losses could be, Job's story helped me remember that God was in control. As coaches, we wanted to win as much as possible and move the program forward . . . quickly! But God's timing is perfect. Looking back, I can see the state of the program when we came to Waco, and the struggles we endured from the scholarship reductions and the suspension from postseason play had some positives. They allowed us to take our time and slowly build the foundation we wanted the program to have. If it had been a different team at a different time, the demands and expectations probably would have also been different. There aren't too many places where you can lose fourteen games in a row and not really worry about your job security. But thankfully, Baylor was one of them. Through Job, my dad and I worked to see the struggle as an opportunity to draw closer to God and trust him more.

Trusting God means trusting that his outcome is perfect. But I think that's aided by looking for and celebrating the wins, however small they might be. For us, those wins were literal, like winning at Purdue. For you, they might be just appreciating some of the people God put in your life to help you through the challenging seasons you encounter.

One of those people for us was Ian McCaw, our athletic director. Not only did Ian work to make sure our program had the resources we needed, but he also prayed regularly for not only our team but for our coaches and their families. You always feel like you have a shot when people, especially your bosses, are praying for you.

> **Trusting God means trusting that his outcome is perfect. But I think that's aided by looking for and celebrating the wins, however small they might be.**

Year three would give me the blessing of drawing even closer—because we struggled even more.

The summer after that second year, the NCAA finished its investigation into Baylor and the problems we'd had leading up to the tragedy. Internally, we had a lot of hope that our response to the inquiry and honesty with the NCAA after the fact might mean we could be moving forward. After all, we'd removed ourselves from postseason play for a year, reduced our available scholarships, and been as cooperative as possible.

In their announcement of their findings, the NCAA said they considered the ultimate punishment: suspension of play for up to two seasons, commonly known as the "death penalty." Only two teams had ever been given that severe a punishment in college athletics history: Southern Methodist's football team and a Division III tennis team. According to the NCAA, we were lucky not to be the third.

The chairman of the NCAA panel leading the investigation, Alabama law professor Gene Marsh, said his committee "walked up to the edge and then stepped back" from giving us the "death penalty." In his statement, Marsh credited Baylor's "honest and very blunt" assessment of the violations and the conditions that led to them. Baylor "took decisive and meaningful action to stop the violations and punish those responsible," Marsh said. "They didn't try to be cute, didn't try to polish the apple."

But they still gave us an additional punishment.

They made us continue to have reduced scholarships for another season, and actually banned us from playing any games outside of our conference in one of the next two seasons.

It was hard. Not "losing your family and livelihood and friends" hard like Job had experienced, but worldly hard. We had just endured two seasons of losing and reduced scholarships and spent two years paying the price for stuff that happened before my family and staff got there. Now we were told it would be worse for the next year.

It looked like I would be spending another season in Job, with Dad.

And in truth, my relationship with God is better for it.

There's no doubt my relationship with Christ grew during that time. When you're on the mountaintop, it's so dangerous because you have so many people praising you—and you think you got to the top of the mountain because of you. And that's when many leaders, in all walks of life, stumble.

When you're in the valley, it can feel very lonely. No one is around to praise you, and you're by yourself. But I think God uses those moments when we are by ourselves, and we don't have anyone else to bring us closer to him.

Many of us only lean on God when he's our only option. Maybe stop and think—that's why he allows us to be in those positions in the first place.

Ideally, you lean on God when you're at the top. But I think it's a lot harder to do if you don't learn to lean on him when you're in the valley. Those first three years, and that third year especially, knowing we would have our time in the desert extended, helped solidify in my own heart the kind of foundation we were trying to build at Baylor.

That reliance on God didn't just come because the results weren't what we wanted on the court.

As a staff, we really tried to see God in everything, even when it wasn't really what we wanted to see. The lack of nonconference games for the 2005–2006 season was going to be tough. And it impacted our program in other ways. For years we'd been selling recruits on this idea of a fresh start and that God was doing amazing things at a program that was dealing with some humbling circumstances. Well, when our circumstances got even more humbling, some of the recruits didn't exactly say "Hallelujah!"

> As a staff, we really tried to see God in everything, even when it wasn't really what we wanted to see.

We lost some recruits when the NCAA sanctions came down. As a staff that tries to invest in relationships, when a recruit chooses to go to a different school, it can be discouraging. When you lose a recruit, you sit up at night and play things back in your mind and ask God, "Why did this happen?" It doesn't make sense.

But a lot of times, God doesn't make sense. That's the point. The Bible tells us to "Trust in the LORD with all your heart and *lean not on your own understanding*; in all your ways submit to him, and he will make your paths straight" (Proverbs 3:5–6, emphasis added).

That's sometimes easier said than done. But our staff was so good about keeping each other accountable in terms of our faith and making sure we intentionally sought God in all of it.

One of the things that Coach Driscoll and Coach Tang would say is, "Do the work and let God decide the results."

If we feel like we haven't put in the work, then that's on us. But if we put in the work, then we have to trust God that he knows what he wants for us, and so it made it a lot easier to not question why people didn't come to the program at a certain time. And it let us be thankful for the chance to move on to the next person and be excited to know that God had the next person in order.

Luckily, God provided the right people. For that 2005 season, we still brought in an incredible recruiting class, despite everything that was happening. Curtis Jerrells and Henry Dugat were highly coveted guards, and Mamadou Diene and Kevin Rogers were both skilled big men. All of them were given the option to be released from their letter of intent as a result of the NCAA sanctions. Thankfully, they stayed true to their word and were willing to go through this last season of struggle. Their commitment would truly establish the foundation for everything that would happen at Baylor.

I think their presence helped us prove to people that we had a bright future. And one of the people who saw it was Tweety Carter.

Born Demond Carter in New Orleans, Tweety got his nickname from his grandmother because of the way he cried as a baby. Tweety would grow to be only about five foot eleven, but he never let his lack of size keep him from being an imposing presence on the court. He started playing high school basketball as a seventh grader in Reserve, Louisiana. By the time he was a ninth grader, he was clearly someone we wanted to be part of what we were building at Baylor.

Now, it isn't like we were the only ones recruiting him. He had schools like Arkansas, Texas, and Kansas checking him out. But one of the things he told me was, those schools that had winning traditions and had put players into the NBA all said he could come to the school and be their next great player. He could be the next Kirk Hinrich. He could be the next T.J. Ford.

Tweety Carter wasn't trying to be the next anyone. He knew God made him to be unique.

His school, Reserve Christian Academy, had never won a state championship before he showed up. By the time he left, they'd won five. He scored seventy-four points in a high school game and was the first McDonald's All-American to commit to our program in school history. He had been part of helping change a program in Louisiana, and so we thought he might be ideal for helping us do it in Texas. When we talked to Tweety, we never sold him on being the next anyone that we had. Quite frankly, we didn't have that many good players for him to emulate.

Tweety committed to us his junior year, while we were stuck not playing any nonconference games. Even better, he never took any other recruiting trips once he committed. That's very rare. But Tweety told us he was committed to us, and he didn't want to see anything else because that might make him waver in his commitment. Why seek something else out if you know what you want?

Tweety's commitment meant a lot to us as a program because it allowed us to show what we were building, or at least trying to, which was attractive to top players. If this kid who was winning state championships and setting all-time high school scoring records was willing to give Baylor a shot, why wouldn't other top players?

The other thing Tweety's commitment showed us was that we could unapologetically talk about God with players. Sometimes, Tweety told us, when certain people would bring up God, it could sound, in Tweety's words, "corny." And it makes sense. If you're cussing out a player in practice or the locker room and then stop and pray before dismissal, you sense how your faith might not resonate in a relatable way.

But at Baylor, we really tried to walk it how we talked it. And, yeah, we might be corny in our own way. We're out here having chapel services with praise music and light shows before games. We're praying before practices. And we're talking about God with the players we're trying to bring into our lives because we want to make sure he is a part of theirs. That's how we were doing things. We were doing the work, and we were trusting God with the results.

And it took a lot of trust. Because the results that third season were pretty bad.

Without nonconference games because of the NCAA sanctions, we just practiced and scrimmaged for months, since our season wouldn't officially start until well after every other team in the country. This made for some pretty monotonous sessions. Practices start in October, and we wouldn't be playing our first game until January. For more than three months, we got really good at practice. Even then, there were some positives.

> **We were doing the work, and we were trusting God with the results.**

Because we were a young team that wasn't as talented as many of the teams in our conference, the extra practice time allowed us to prepare our young players more than they otherwise might've. It also allowed us to get creative.

Sometimes we wouldn't play basketball at practice. Weeks of practicing at a time with no games in between can be frustrating and make you want to throw things. Sometimes we played dodgeball. We also tried to give our kids the excuse to get out of town since they weren't traveling to any tournaments or road games against nonconference teams. So we set up a practice scrimmage in Dallas at American Airlines Arena, where the NBA's Dallas Mavericks play. We rode the bus, stayed overnight, and did the whole walk-through routine to try to prepare our new players, and old ones, for our first game of the season, which was a road game against Bobby Knight and Texas Tech.

Imagine you're driving and about to enter onto a freeway. As you're preparing to merge into traffic, it's helpful to be going the same speed as the cars that are already driving on that road, right? Well, the game at Texas Tech was like trying to merge onto the highway after we had just started the car. For as much as we'd been practicing, our engine was really just getting warmed up; Texas Tech's was already going full speed.

We lost by eighteen. And over the next four games we lost by an average of more than twenty points. Teams play nonconference games for a reason.

Losing is never fun, and losing by a lot is even less fun. But at least we were playing. And our freshmen were getting better. After a close loss at Texas A&M, we actually won two of our next three games. We then had a brutal four-game stretch that included losses at Oklahoma, Texas, and Kansas, which all finished the season ranked in the top 25.

We had two home games left, against Iowa State and then Coach Knight and Texas Tech. We really tried to emphasize to our players, who were coming down the home stretch of an incredibly challenging and unique season, that we wanted to finish on a high note. Our chapels before those home games were on finishing our race well. We could all sense that things were changing. The first two years we'd been severely undermanned, with only six or seven scholarship players available. But that wasn't now.

Now we had a really good shooter in Aaron Bruce. We had a scorer in Curtis Jerrells and senior leadership in Tommy Swanson. And we had a big guy in Mamadou, who could make our defense much better. We might still have been David in the eyes of the rest of the teams, but we had more than one stone in our slingshot. We'd practiced too long, worked too hard, and played enough dodgeball. We could win these games.

We got up on Iowa State early and beat them by nineteen. It was by far our biggest win in Big 12 play since our staff had been there. Against Texas Tech and Coach Knight, we were down by four at halftime, but we knew we could play better. Aaron Bruce told his teammates we weren't going to lose the game, and then he went out and made six threes in the second half.

We won by eleven. It was the first time we had won back-to-back games since I'd been there, and with four wins, it was our best conference record yet.

Yes, we only won four games and lost thirteen for the season. And since we didn't play any nonconference games, the record books show that 2006 season as one of the worst in school history with only four wins. It was, without a doubt, a valley.

But being in that locker room after the Texas Tech game, and being with those players throughout that season, we knew God was working.

And we felt like we had better days ahead.

NINE

PROCESS OVER PROGRESS

Whatever you do, work at it with all your heart, as working for the Lord, not for human masters.

COLOSSIANS 3:23

By the fall of 2006, I was starting my fourth year as the head coach at Baylor. And in some ways it felt like we were established and settled in as Waco residents. Kelly and I loved being parents, and watching Mackenzie grow up in our new home for the past two years was a source of joy regardless of what was happening on the court. Our coaching staff of Jerome Tang, Mark Morefield, Matt Driscoll, Paul Mills, and Stephen Brough had established a rhythm and relationship with one another that made working every day a joy.

But in a lot of ways, it felt like we were just getting started.

Because of the legacy of the NCAA violations and subsequent sanctions, our fourth season at Baylor was going to be the first one where we felt like we would be competing on a level playing field. Yes, we had been there for three years. But this would be the first one where we had as many scholarship players as everyone else. And we felt good about those players.

We had had three top-twenty recruiting classes in a row, so we felt that we had the talent. But even though we had ten players coming back, we were still really young. We had our Australian assassin, Aaron Bruce, and last year's talented freshmen, Mamadou Diene, Curtis Jerrells, Henry Dugat, and Kevin Rogers, were now sophomores. Plus we were bringing in Tweety Carter and two more freshmen, Josh Lomers and Penny Thiam, in what was considered the seventeenth best recruiting class in the country.

We had worked hard to build a team that would give our fans something to cheer for on the court. These fans, after all, were at times cheering for five walk-ons just a few years ago. So it was nice to think that the people who spent their time and money to see us play would be able to experience more victories now that the sanctions were behind us. The year before we didn't even get to start playing until January. At least this year our fans could see us play for a full season.

But we also wanted our players to represent our values even when no one was looking.

Not that all of our players were saints. As my wife can tell you, I'm not one either.

That's one area where being surrounded by men of faith really helped me. When you recruit, you're looking at things like wingspan and jump shots. But you're also trying to see if this kid will go to class. What will he be doing on Saturday nights?

Just because a player says he's a Christian doesn't mean the answers to those questions will be good ones. Two of the players on our team that year, Mamadou Diene and Penny Thiam, were Muslim and were some of our players with the highest character.

When we were recruiting Mamadou and Penny, I remember asking Pastor Wible for guidance. We wanted to honor their culture and their religious beliefs, but we also did not want to moderate our message. Pastor Wible helped us see that even though Mamadou and

Penny didn't share our faith, they shared our values. And to be clear, they were really good players. We felt like God had blessed us with the chance to bring the right people into the team; now we had to go out and show what we could do.

By our fifth game, we had already won as many games as we did the previous season, with our only loss in that stretch coming at Gonzaga. When nonconference play had ended, we were 10–3, already with more wins than any of our previous three teams. Our first conference game was at Oklahoma State, which was ranked No. 12, and when we only lost by four, it felt like maybe we were turning a corner.

It ended up being more like a really long curve.

That's where being immersed in a community of faith can make a difference. Whenever you're going through a challenging time, when life just isn't happening the way you want, many people try to take things into their own hands. Instead, God wants us to keep seeking and trusting him. Keep studying the Bible. Keep praying. Keep asking your friends for their prayers. Eventually, something will happen, even if it's just you seeing why God has you in that season.

Having our coaches be men of faith helped us aspire toward that mentality. Not that it made the losing any easier.

We beat Texas Tech and Colorado at home, but those would prove to be exceptions rather than the rule. We lost nine of our first eleven conference games, and now a team that seemed headed for a record above .500, and eligibility in postseason play was in danger of falling short once again. Our talent had been on display on many occasions. Unfortunately, so had our youth. But coming off close losses at home to Oklahoma and at Missouri, we had a big matchup with Texas up next. At a record of 12–12, it was important for us to stem the tide and allow our players to experience a big win. As a young team, one of the hardest things to do is make the one or two plays that are the difference between a close loss and an important win. Texas would provide that opportunity.

As the biggest school in the state, Texas was everyone's rival. Or at least a team everyone wanted to beat. That year's team featured a freshman phenom, Kevin Durant, who would go on to be the No. 2 pick in the NBA draft and win multiple NBA championships. A six-foot-ten forward, Durant played more like a guard and was an excellent shooter.

We knew going into the game that stopping him would be our biggest challenge and the key to getting the biggest win of the season—as well as our biggest win during our time at Baylor. It was a Saturday night, and the Ferrell Center was packed. The crowd was into it, and we came out with one of our best efforts of the season.

We held Durant to only one three-pointer that game, but he made nine free throws and finished with twenty points. But at the end, we were in the game. We had the ball, down one with only a few seconds to go. We weren't supposed to be in this game, but we were. Our players could sense that this might be their moment. The only problem was our two centers, Mamadou Diene and Josh Lomers, both fouled out. We had our third-stringer, Mark Shepherd, in the game. Now, Mark's hand was pretty banged up, and he had a sizable bandage on it. In truth, he shouldn't have been in the game, but with our other big men fouled out we really didn't have any choice.

We drew up a play that we thought might give us a chance to win the game. But Texas coach Rick Barnes had his team prepared, and as our team came down, Texas forced a pass. The only person open was Mark, who caught the ball and with time winding down, rose up and shot the ball, bandaged hand and all. The ball rimmed out.

We lost by one.

I know it's just a game, but sometimes sports can be draining. Our crowd let out one of those audible groans, and they pretty much spoke for the entire Waco area. Our team was obviously incredibly disappointed. But as coaches, it's our job to keep their heads up and tell them to get some rest, and get ready for the next game. But my next game would come earlier than theirs.

Looking back, it probably would have made sense to check the basketball schedule before I signed up, but when I got home that night after the game, I saw a reminder that it was my turn in our church children's nursery with Kelly the next day. So, as dispiriting as the loss was, my next game was eight hours later, hanging out with my daughter, Mackenzie, and the other two-year-olds in the nursery.

Pastor Wible walked by, stuck his head in, and expressed some surprise to see me drawing up plays with the kids. Having a game come down to our third-string center with a nearly broken hand wasn't really how we had hoped the last play would go. But dealing with some of the "accidents" in the nursery the next morning helped me get past it. Kind of.

We split our last four games of the season, meaning we entered the Big 12 tournament needing to win two games to be eligible for the NIT. If we won the whole tournament, we would qualify for the NCAA tournament. As a coach, you're always motivating your players. "Look, guys," we would say, "we are four wins away from making the big dance."

We beat Missouri in the first round of the Big 12 tournament by sixteen, setting up a second-round matchup, and rematch, with Texas.

Win the game and we knew we were advancing not only in the Big 12 tournament but also in the status of the program. The team had made the NIT in 2001, and that was the first postseason appearance in the last thirteen years. Baylor basketball didn't really go to the postseason. For us to have a chance to do it, just four years after everything that had happened and one year after we won four games in an entire, albeit abbreviated, season? This was our opportunity. And we went out to seize it.

We jumped on Texas early, partly because Durant was missing, and went into halftime up eighteen. We were close. We stressed to the players not to relax, and that a team with as much talent would be fighting back. We were right.

We expanded our lead to twenty in the first few minutes of the second half, but then Kevin Durant gave us, and the rest of the basketball world, a preview of what he could do. Durant scored twenty-six in the second half, and D.J. Augustin hit a basket and some free throws in the final seconds to close it out. We lost by five, and our season was over.

The locker room after the game was sad but not despondent. One advantage of being a young team is that you still have more time to play, to grow, and to win. Being that close just gave us a taste of what we knew was possible if we just worked harder and stayed together.

That off-season, we healed from the heartbreak of just missing the postseason. And we came out for the next season ready to prove just how strong we were. It turned out we had healed really well.

Of course, things don't always go as you planned. In October 2007, I had to leave Big 12 media day early, flying back from Kansas City, because Kelly was in labor with our second child, and first son, Peyton.

Peyton was our family's newest addition, but I was really excited about the returning players too.

All of our young players had now gained experience. We really came out to show we were ready to take that next step. We beat Notre Dame and South Carolina in big nonconference games early, and we won our first three Big 12 games to start the 2007–2008 season 15–2. We were rolling. We even were ranked for the first time in thirty-nine years, coming in at No. 25 in the polls. For a team not used to success, being ranked, even as the last team in the top twenty-five, was a really big deal. But being ranked is one thing. Staying ranked is another. And our first game as a ranked team was going to be at our rival's Texas A&M in College Station.

For a team that had to wait thirty-nine years to be ranked, it figured that our first game as a top 25 team would also take a while. As in, five overtimes.

Five of our players fouled out, so it became a game of attrition. And just when you thought we might be about to win, they'd hit a shot or something and here came the next overtime. The game lasted so long that after the third overtime, one of the referees came over and was confused about which overtime period was starting. He thought it was the third, and when told the fourth one was up next, he just shook his head and walked back to the court. Luckily, our players stayed focused. We were in excellent shape, thanks in large part to Charlie Melton, who I believe is the best strength coach in the country.

Curtis Jerrells scored eleven in the fifth extra period, finishing with thirty-six for the game, and we had won our first game as a ranked team in four decades.

It was a nice feeling. But playing that much basketball and exerting that much physical and emotional effort took its toll. We lost six of the next seven games, and all of a sudden, not only were we not ranked anymore, but we were sliding out of the NCAA tournament projections.

Our latest loss had come at Oklahoma in overtime—of course—and our team's spirit was suddenly not so good. At practice later that week we were having a hard time keeping the players motivated. As coaches, the one thing we can control is our energy. But it's also our job to try to use our energy to motivate energy and performance out of our players. Well, when you're on a losing streak, that's harder to do. Luckily, inspiration came from Coach Driscoll and his infrequent grooming habits.

At practice, some of the players were giving Coach Driscoll a hard time about how long he was letting his hair get. Never one to let a motivational moment go to waste, Coach Driscoll told them that he would let them cut his hair however they wanted. All they had to do was win a game.

After we won at Kansas State, which featured Freshman All-American Michael Beasley, our postgame celebration was a little different: the players shaved Coach Driscoll's head. Coach Dris isn't a vain guy, but I'm not sure he'd ever been prouder of his appearance than that night. And now that they had a taste for not only barbering but winning, they wanted more. After each game the players called out a different assistant, and the coaches dutifully, if not enthusiastically, let the players shave their heads. We won four of our next five games to get back into the projected field for the NCAA tournament.

We lost in the first round of the Big 12 tournament but still were being projected as a team that should make the sixty-four-team tournament by ESPN's Joe Lunardi. The bracket was always unveiled on the Sunday evening telecast that aired on CBS. We felt good enough about our chances that we held a tournament selection show watch party at our arena and invited the families and supporters of the team and players to attend. For their part, CBS sent a camera crew to film our reactions when we found out that we did, or didn't, make the field.

The NCAA tournament bracket is divided into four regions: East, South, Midwest, and West. CBS, which always carries not only the tournament but the famed "Selection Sunday" broadcast in which the bracket is revealed, discloses the names of the teams by region. They'll show the top half of the East bracket and then the bottom. Then the top half of the South, and so on, until they get to the last half of the last region.

When the broadcast began, CBS showed the East bracket first. Of the sixteen teams they announced, none of them wore our green and gold. But, hey, still forty-eight more teams to go. Then they showed the South, and we weren't included. Half of the bracket was left, but half of it was also now gone. We were going to make it, right? I mean "Joey Brackets" Lunardi himself said we were in, so we had to be, right?

The Midwest bracket was up next. Once again, we weren't included. At this point, I was worried. Making matters worse, CBS cut to commercial before unveiling the last region.

I don't know what I would consider some of the most awkward moments of my life. I'm sure there were a couple of times with Kelly when we were dating when I made it weird. But sitting in an arena filled with fans of the team you coach, based on the quickly unraveling idea that you're going to make the NCAA tournament for the first time in thirty years, and waiting for the commercial break to be over so you can see if you've invited all these people over for nothing is kind of up there.

When the broadcast resumed, CBS showed the top half of the West region. Again, no Baylor. Then they showed three of the remaining four matchups, none of which featured us.

To say I was praying to God fervently in this moment would be an understatement.

Finally, they showed the last game, and last two teams, to be included in the 2008 tournament. After showing No. 6 seed Purdue, CBS host Greg Gumbel said, "We know they're sitting around wondering if they're going to make it. As the eleven seed in the West, the Baylor Bears, making their first trip to the NCAA tournament since 1988."

I'd like to say I reacted calmly, like that image of Larry Bird when Reggie Miller hit a game winner against the Chicago Bulls in the playoffs. I'd like to say that I stood up, gave Kelly a hug and my kids a kiss on the forehead, picked up Peyton out of his stroller and gave him a warm embrace, and then politely high-fived my players and staff.

What actually happened was I jumped up, screaming like a lunatic. We all went crazy.

It's on video, so the reaction is there for anyone to verify. But I definitely jumped out of my seat, pumped my fist in the air a few times, did a quick dogpile onto my staff, then remembered that I am in fact an adult man in his late thirties with a wife and kids and made my way over to Kelly and Mackenzie for a hug. I also made sure to thank God. He did it. Of course God would have us make it as the last team. We had to play so many extra minutes that season in some of our biggest wins, why not wait the longest of any team in the country to find out we were included?

I think when you look back and you see extreme circumstances or dramatic moments, you can see God. God is in the mundane and everyday stuff also, but it can be easy to overlook or forget that God's in charge all the time in the normalcy of life. So those moments when things get tough or you get stressed, I think God uses those times to help remind us that we need him.

> I think when you look back and you see extreme circumstances or dramatic moments, you can see God.

Helping take a program from the brink of the NCAA "death penalty" into the NCAA tournament in five seasons was the kind of thing that God had to be involved in. As coaches, it was humbling to know God was using us to do a thing that would glorify him. Our making the tournament was the kind of thing that would bring more attention to our school, our story, and our God. It was an amazing feeling of accomplishment.

But we felt like our story was just beginning.

TEN

CHASE LIONS

Trust in the LORD with all your heart and lean not on your
own understanding.

PROVERBS 3:5

We traveled to Washington, DC, for the first-round game against Purdue. Being in the Big 12, we had played in big games before, even ones on national television. But we had never played in the NCAA tournament. And I'd only been the head coach in one NIT game before. Before the game, in the locker room, we prayed and thanked God for the opportunity to represent him on the national stage and for being faithful all the time, in wins and losses. We asked him to give us strength and courage for the battle head.

We should have asked him to help us play defense.

Purdue, normally a slower-paced team, seemed quite content to run up and down the court with us. And the way they were shooting, who could blame them? We went into the half down by nineteen, and though we came out with better effort and attention to detail in the second half, we lost by eleven.

It wasn't the performance that we wanted, but at the same time the team had accomplished a tremendous amount. We told the players after the game how proud we were of them and their accomplishments and how proud they should and could be of what they had done.

For players like Aaron Bruce and Mark Shepherd, they'd played their last game in a Baylor uniform. I told them how grateful we were for their willingness to take a chance on us, on themselves, and on Baylor. They helped establish the foundation for our ascension to an NCAA tournament team. Now they were graduating and moving on to the next phases of their lives and careers.

We were looking ahead too.

We lost Aaron and Mark, but we were bringing a lot of talent back. Curtis Jerrells, Kevin Rogers, Henry Dugat, and Mamadou Diene were seniors, Tweety Carter was a junior, and LaceDarius Dunn was a sophomore. We felt that we had talented experience on the team. Plus, we were coming off of our first tournament appearance in thirty years, so as we went into the next season, expectations were high.

Summers for college basketball coaches are the one time of the year when things can slow down a little bit; we can take vacations with our families, and we have some recruiting dead periods where we aren't allowed to make contact with high school players, so we can rest and recharge. But not everyone on our staff unplugs.

Pastor Wible spent that summer praying and fasting, seeking God's wisdom for the themes and messages he would be delivering for that season's chapel services. That's one thing we as a staff take a lot of pride in. Yes, we develop plans for our practices and scouting reports for our opponents. But we also spend time thinking and praying about our pregame chapel services and what we feel like our players need to hear from God.

One thing I've learned is, don't think of the pursuit of God as a last-minute or quick thing to check off your list. You can do that. But

God wants our time and our hearts. The more of those we give him, the more he will do in our lives.

As part of his process, Pastor Wible told me that while fasting and praying, he had been having dreams about Benaiah from the Old Testament and felt like we were going to be facing a lion, just like him.

Now, if you've never heard of Benaiah, you're probably not alone. Benaiah is mentioned in several Old Testament books as a commander in David's army, and in both 2 Samuel and 1 Chronicles he is mentioned as having done some mighty things, including killing a giant Egyptian warrior with his own spear. But it also says that he killed a lion in a pit on a snowy day.

> **God wants our time and our hearts. The more of those we give him, the more he will do in our lives.**

In the Bible, the reference to the pit means that Benaiah didn't have an escape route. You go into a pit with a lion; you have to kill or be killed. And the fact that it was snowing is meant to show that the lion would have been especially fierce, since the lion would have been especially hungry in snowy weather as less food would have been freely roaming.

The point is, Benaiah was a tough man.

According to Pastor Wible, we were going to be Benaiah this season. Specifically, he told me he had a dream that we were going to play the Lions for a national title. Which is great—I mean a championship? Let's go!

Now, I'm an optimist by nature, but given that we hadn't won a postseason game since 1950, the odds of us making the championship game seemed fairly long. Also, who are the Lions? Penn State was the only team named the Lions that we could come up with, and they probably had less NCAA postseason history than we did. So, as much as I respected Pastor Wible and his prayerful fasting and pursuit of God, I'm not sure how much faith I had in the prediction.

Sometimes it's good to be reminded that I just coach basketball for a living.

Pastor Wible did his part and bought some glass lions to hand out to the team that fall. And as we began practicing, and into the season, we gave every player a lion and encouraged the team to be brave like Benaiah. We'd earned the right to fight the lion last season by making the tournament. Now we wanted to do something great. We weren't going to be afraid. We were going to chase that lion into the snowy pit.

When our season started, it looked like Pastor Wible might have been onto something. We started 15–3 and were ranked in the top 20 nationally for the first time in our program's history. It felt like things were going according to plan. Our talented players were elevating the program to new heights, and we seemed to be building momentum for where we felt like God wanted us to be.

At least, it seemed like that.

We won three of our first four Big 12 games, including our first two at home in the Ferrell Center. Inside, I was telling myself that the NCAA was a real possibility. One of the things that making the NCAA tournament does for your program is it gives it additional visibility not only nationally but in your own backyard as well. Suddenly, Baylor basketball games were cool to go to, if for no other reason than other people were going also. And so, in those first two Big 12 games in Waco, we had more than eight thousand people in the stands, and they were loud the whole time. I still wasn't sure how we were going to play the Lions for a championship, but we were winning more than we ever had before and were ranked in the top 20 for the first time in program history. So the championship part of it didn't seem that outlandish.

Then, adversity hit. By adversity, I mean the Big 12 schedule.

In our next six games, we played Texas, Kansas, and Oklahoma twice, plus two road games in tough venues at Missouri and at Texas Tech. Some of them were close, but we lost them all. The Texas game was especially tough since we were still looking for our first win as a staff against the Longhorns, but we lost by six, bringing our conference record to 3–3. It wouldn't get any better for the rest of the season.

After we lost six straight games, we rebounded to beat Texas A&M in front of a packed house in Waco. That was awesome, and our players really responded to the belief and energy from the fans when we needed it the most. Plus, our fans always like seeing us beat our rivals from College Station. But then we lost three of our next four, and so we came to our last game of the season, at home against Nebraska at 5–10 in conference play and 17–12 overall. Our chances of making the NCAA tournament were basically over unless we could win the upcoming Big 12 tournament. But for that Nebraska game, which was senior night, we were hoping the fans and team could celebrate the journey the players had led us on over the past four years. Guys like Curtis Jerrells, Mamadou Diene, Kevin Rogers, and Henry Dugat took a chance on us when it wasn't all that clear what Baylor basketball would look like.

Especially Curtis; he was a kid from Austin who committed to us in March of that first year on the job and was the first commit to us in that recruiting class. He stayed with his commitment even when he found out we had another year of probation for what became his freshman season. And as a highly ranked recruit, having him as a commit helped us convince other talented players that what we were building at Baylor was different from what had been there before.

It would have been fitting for our fans to come out and cheer what Curtis and the rest of that first full class had done for the program, even if the results this season hadn't been all that great.

But that isn't how it worked out.

We had one of the smallest crowds of the year, and we ended up losing, at home, to Nebraska in our last regular season game. The result was disappointing, but mostly I was disappointed for the experience that our seniors had. Because the players who had come to play for us and who helped change our whole culture deserved to be celebrated. After all they'd done and been through, we felt that they deserved better.

The locker room after the game was quiet. This wasn't how we saw the season after our breakthrough appearance working out. We thought we were going to play for a championship, against Lions, in the snow. Well, our losses had stacked up, the championship hopes were virtually nonexistent, and the spring weather was approaching. We didn't see much snow on the horizon.

Before the season, we always assign responsibilities for not only which coaches will be doing which scouting assignments for which games ahead of time but which coaches will be doing which chapel services ahead of which road games. Coach Mills was in charge of the pregame services for the Big 12 tournament in Oklahoma City. So, going into this tournament, Coach Mills had wanted to focus on a verse from 2 Chronicles that says, "For the eyes of the LORD range throughout the earth to strengthen those whose hearts are fully committed to him" (16:9).

For us, on the back end of what had been a disappointing campaign, there were a lot of things we couldn't control. We couldn't control all the games we had lost earlier in the season. We couldn't control which other teams we would have to play in the Big 12 tournament, or any postseason tournament if we qualified for one. But we could control our hearts and ask God to make sure that they were fully committed to him. Coach Mills asked our team to be committed to that, to be committed to God, and just trust that results on and off the court would take care of themselves.

Because we had such a poor finish to the season, we actually had to play in the Wednesday game, which was reserved for some of the lower-seeded teams. So, to win the tournament and go to the NCAA tournament, we would have to win four games in four days—something no team had ever done in the Big 12 tournament.

Our first game was actually a rematch with Nebraska. And four days after they had beaten us on our senior night, we returned the favor, winning by fifteen. For a team that had lost eight of its last ten games, it was nice to feel like maybe we were starting a different kind of streak. Of course, up next was another challenge of biblical proportions, at least in terms of the college basketball world: Kansas.

Kansas is an iconic name in the college basketball nation. Dr. James Naismith, the man credited with creating basketball, coached at Kansas. Naismith was followed by Phog Allen, who is considered the father of basketball coaching. Larry Brown coached there. He was followed by Roy Williams. Now they had Bill Self, who was well on his way to becoming a Hall of Fame coach in his own right.

For this chapel service, Coach Mills read from 1 Samuel 16. God had tasked Samuel with selecting a new king, and he had gone to Jesse's house to see his seven sons. After seeing the oldest son, Samuel thought, *Surely, this is the one the Lord has anointed.* But the Lord spoke to Samuel, and reminded him, "The LORD does not look at the things people look at. People look at the outward appearance, but the LORD looks at the heart" (v. 7).

At the end of this story, Samuel looked past all the bigger, stronger brothers and was told to select David, because his heart was the one that was after the Lord's.

As we've discussed, David went on to do many things, including slaying Goliath. If people want to see Kansas as Goliath in this scenario, have at it. They were the top seed, coming off multiple days of rest while we had played the day before. Again, those weren't things we could control. But we could control our collective heart.

Our heart was good enough to help us beat Kansas by seven, the first victory for Baylor over the Jayhawks since we arrived as the coaching staff. We built a big lead, and, as in previous big games, we let the other team back in, and we actually trailed by five in the second half before LaceDarius Dunn hit a bunch of three-pointers and helped us pull off the upset. It was an awesome feeling. Kansas was the three-time defending champion of the tournament. But like David's, our aim had been true. However, David got to rest after slaying one giant. We had another one on deck: Texas was waiting in the semifinals.

Now, as a staff we hadn't beaten Texas. But that was okay, because the school hadn't beaten them since 1999. We'd lost twenty-four straight games to the Longhorns. Compared to them, we were definitely the weaker clan. So in the pregame chapel service, Coach Mills talked to us about Gideon and how he feared he wouldn't be able to conquer the Midianite army. "But Lord!" Gideon cried out to God in the book of Judges. "How can I deliver Israel? Just look! My clan is the weakest in Manasseh, and I am the youngest in my family" (Judges 6:15, author's paraphrase).

Well, our program was way less established, our players not as highly regarded as recruits, our coaches less respected, and our team was playing its third game in three days while Texas was only playing its second. We were weaker. But we were also asking God to be with us.

We beat Texas by six, taking the lead for good when Tweety passed to LaceDarius for a three-pointer with a minute left. We had made it to the first Big 12 championship game in program history.

Unfortunately, Coach Mills's pregame chapel service must not have been as good as the ones beforehand, since we lost to Missouri in the Big 12 championship game. Just kidding.

The reality was, four games in four days was a lot, and in the second half our legs gave out against Mike Anderson's Missouri team, which was pressing and running us the entire game. Good strategy by them, bad luck for us. And coming up one game shy of another trip to the NCAA tournament was tough to take. It really seemed like God was up to something. Which, of course, he was. It just wasn't the thing we wanted or were expecting.

That will happen sometimes.

The Bible tells us that God's ways are not our ways, and we can't begin to comprehend them. By definition, that means sometimes things will happen that you don't understand. But does that mean God isn't working in your life? As Paul would say, "By no means!"

In this case, God took our disappointment and delivered a reminder about faithfulness.

We didn't make the NCAAs, but we qualified for the NIT. We were selected to host a first-round match against Georgetown, a really famous program that had gone to the Final Four in 2007 and was led by John Thompson III. And since we had gone on our run in the Big 12 tournament, our fans had gotten reenergized and reengaged. So when Georgetown came to Waco, Waco came out to see it.

> **The Bible tells us that God's ways are not our ways, and we can't begin to comprehend them. By definition, that means sometimes things will happen that you don't understand.**

Don't get me wrong; it would have been awesome to make the NCAA tournament again. But by not making it, we got a marquee name to come play us on our home court, which never would have happened otherwise. We also got to have a packed house in the Ferrell Center to see our seniors off in the way we felt they deserved. And when we beat Georgetown 74–72 in that first-round game, our fans and our seniors, two groups that had been through so much in the past few years of Baylor basketball, got to celebrate the program's first postseason win since 1950 together.

Amen.

After the Georgetown game, we went to Virginia Tech. We won that one by eighteen. For the quarterfinal game, we traveled to Auburn and won a nail-biter of a game, with Curtis hitting a free throw with six seconds left to help us win by two. We were in the semifinals.

Like the NCAA, the NIT has a Final Four, only theirs is always in New York City at Madison Square Garden. We had a game against San Diego State, which we won by fourteen. So, now, in a matter of a little more than three weeks, we had gone from a demoralizing loss on our home court for senior night to one game away from a championship. Our opponent in that championship game?

Penn State University. Also known as the Nittany Lions.

Honestly, at the time we couldn't really believe it. Of course, Pastor Wible was back in Texas, but even he was overwhelmed by the sense of God's hand in it all.

We didn't beat Penn State. We trailed most of the second half and lost by four. I'd be lying if I said we weren't disappointed to lose in another championship game in a couple weeks. Of course we wanted to win. As Herman Edwards has so famously pointed out, you play to win the game.

But God isn't less good because we lost. He's as good in our losses as he is in our wins. And I think a sign of spiritual maturity is seeing God in all parts of the game, regardless of the result.

> **A sign of spiritual maturity is seeing God in all parts of the game, regardless of the result.**

We didn't beat the Lions for a championship. But we did play them, as Pastor Wible dreamed we would. And it wasn't snowing in New York that April when we were there.

But as Coach Driscoll pointed out, Penn State wasn't that far away from New York City, and they bussed thirteen or fourteen loads of students in for the game. And guess what color they wore for the final? White. So, in some ways, we sort of did play in a snowy pit against the Lions. God did that.

After the tournament, Coach Mills was telling his brother about it, and his brother wanted to know what part of the Bible the story of Benaiah was in. Again, it isn't the most commonly referenced story out there. In fact, Coach Mills himself didn't know, so he called Coach Tang to look it up. Coach Tang was in his hotel room in New York, so he got out the Bible in his room, and when he opened it up, there was only one marker in the Bible.

The marker was in the book of 2 Samuel, chapter 23, verse 20.

The story was about Benaiah and his battle with a lion.

It would have been nice to win the NIT. But moments like that remind you that if you're playing for God, regardless of what the scoreboard says, you can't lose.

ELEVEN

GAIN FAITH WHILE LOSING THE WORLD

Do not be anxious about anything, but in every situation, by prayer and petition, with thanksgiving, present your requests to God.

PHILIPPIANS 4:6

Losing in the NIT Finals was disappointing. But we were excited to have experienced God showing up.

When you regularly pursue God, it's important to stop and see the ways he is speaking and moving in your life, even if the ultimate outcome isn't yet what you've hoped for. Celebrating God's presence in your life and the impact he is having is another way of drawing closer to him.

For us, that experience of feeling as though God was moving in our lives made us more excited to see what he could do next. And we felt like we had some really nice tools for him to work

> **Celebrating God's presence in your life and the impact he is having is another way of drawing closer to him.**

with. Even though we were picked to finish tenth in the Big 12 pre-season coaches' poll, we liked our team and felt that, after making the NCAA tournament in 2008 and then the NIT Finals in 2009, we had a chance to take the next step as a program. Tweety Carter and Josh Lomers were back for their senior years, LaceDarius Dunn was a junior, and we added Ekpe Udoh as a transfer from Michigan, and Quincy Acy and Anthony Jones were back as sophomores. We'd had talent before, but this year's team seemed to be maybe the most balanced in terms of experience and potential at every position.

Being picked to finish so low in the conference only added fuel and motivation to our players. We always tried to keep it positive in practice, but we also let them know what other people thought. And, for whatever reason, it seemed to work. We got off to an amazing start, entering conference play at 12–1. But after the dramatic slide we'd experienced the previous year, we wanted to stay focused and keep our heads down. By the time we picked them up at the end of the regular season, we were 11–5 in conference, good enough to tie for the second-best record in the league.

So much for those coaches' predictions.

We lost in the semifinals of the Big 12 tournament, but we knew we would make March Madness. After the year before, we felt ready for the challenge of winning our first ever NCAA tournament game as a staff, and the first one at Baylor since 1950.

We earned a 3 seed, which of course just makes you nervous for the Cinderella upset you might be facing. And our opponent, Sam Houston State, made it close. They actually led in the second half, and we were tied with three minutes to go, but Quincy Acy and LaceDarius Dunn finished what Ekpe started, and we won by nine.

The postgame locker room was pretty surreal. Six years earlier we had celebrated winning one conference game. Now we had won our first NCAA tournament game in six decades. I was late to my postgame media session, but I had a good excuse—we celebrated in the locker room for a while.

Our team was hitting its stride. Ekpe was showing the kind of talent and athleticism we thought he could when he joined us, and we won our next game against Old Dominion in the second round, and then we beat St. Mary's in the Sweet 16. We were in the Elite 8, one win away from a Final Four appearance.

Standing in our way was Duke.

We actually played the game in Houston, so we felt like we had something of a home court advantage, at least geographically. Then when our bus arrived at Reliant Stadium, we knew we would have the advantage in terms of support too. Baylor Nation turned out! We saw green and gold everywhere and found out later that the attendance of 47,492 was the second-largest crowd to attend a regional final ever.

For the first time, it felt as though Baylor basketball had arrived. And we wanted to give them something to cheer for.

We were up two with four minutes to go when we found Quincy Acy for what looked like an and-one basket that would have sent him to the line to put us up five and foul out their center, Brian Zoubek. Instead, the official called it a charge on Quincy, which gave the ball back to Duke . . . and instead fouled out Quincy, one of our big guys. From there, Duke outscored us 15–3 over the next three and a half minutes. The game was over.

No one wanted to use the charge call as an excuse. Some of the national media people told me and wrote that it looked like Zoubek got to the spot late and it should have been called in our favor. Obviously, it would have been nice if we had gotten the call. Sometimes close calls go your way, and sometimes they don't. There's nothing you can do. I chose to focus our discussion on something we could control: we should have defended and rebounded better down the stretch and didn't.

Losing like that was incredibly frustrating. Duke would go on to win the national title, the fourth in Coach Krzyzewski's career. To be as close as we were to winning that game made me realize how good we could be. But then I had some new challenges to worry about.

Some time earlier, we became aware of some allegations that the NCAA was investigating regarding our recruiting practices. The investigation, which would eventually span three years, included a review of over nine hundred thousand telephone calls and text messages sent by staff of Baylor men's and women's basketball. The way the NCAA tracks and counts phone calls requires the initial call or voice mail to be logged, even if no contact is actually made. Failure to do so then causes each additional call or text to be counted, even if the NCAA wouldn't have counted it had the initial call been properly catalogued.

In truth, we did a bad job of tracking the communications, which made our numbers appear to be in violation of the NCAA's guidelines. Eventually, I appreciated the support that came from people like CBS Sports' Gary Parrish, who, when everything was concluded, wrote, "The biggest thing the NCAA was able to charge Baylor with after a lengthy investigation is that the staff got kinda crazy with their iPhones, which should be cause for a massive party in Waco provided those at the Christian school hold massive parties."

For the record—we do party in Waco. We even dance too.

But while the investigation was underway, no one felt much like partying or dancing.

In fact, facing allegations of wrongdoing was one of the most trying times of my professional career for several reasons.

You know how sometimes you will hear politicians say, "I can't comment on that because of the nature of the investigation"? Well, when the NCAA is involved, that's absolutely the case. You couldn't talk about it at all because if you do share any information, you can get in more trouble with the NCAA. So, really, Kelly became the only person I could talk to about what was happening. I couldn't talk with Coach Tang about it because that would have been a violation, and if he was ever asked about anything under oath, he would have to tell the truth. I couldn't talk to my brother, Bryce, who was an assistant at Valpo, about it for the same reason. Even at church, the only thing I could really say was that I would appreciate prayer, but I couldn't share what I was asking others to pray for.

In that time, not being able to talk about things with my closest friends and family was incredibly isolating, which only made dealing with it harder. Luckily, Kelly is a spiritual rock. Looking back, she would say now that the time of the investigation made our marriage stronger because it forced us to rely on God and each other.

Roughly 50 percent of marriages today end in divorce. But for couples who pray together, few end that way. We always try to, but Kelly and I prayed together consistently during that time. And I don't think it's an accident that our marriage felt stronger during that season as a result. Ultimately, the investigation was something I could only talk to Kelly and God about.

> **Sometimes, the things we think are standing in our way are actually pushing us toward God's desires for our lives.**

Sometimes, the things we think are standing in our way are actually pushing us toward God's desires for our lives. If you find yourself in a similar situation, try to think that God has given you exactly what you need to endure and manage the challenge you're facing.

For me, God gave me Kelly.

Unfortunately, while I couldn't talk about the investigation, other people could. Many reporters, picking up the rumor of the investigation, ran with the story and the idea that "Scott Drew and the Baylor Baptists were cheaters."

Now, no one likes being called names, especially if it means having your reputation and your integrity questioned. But one thing my wife and the coaches on our staff helped me keep in mind was that these people out there writing negative things about us didn't really know us.

One guy wrote an article that said, "Scott Drew walks around with a Bible in one hand and money for recruits in the other."

It wasn't true, of course, but it didn't make it easier to read. To most of the reporters' credit, whenever they wrote something like that, I would call them and just say, "Hey—we don't know each other," and try to give them some accurate information as far as I could.

Mostly, they were receptive, and even if they didn't walk back what they wrote, they would at least know next time where we were coming from. You can't control other people, but you can control the way you react and respond to them. Not that it was always easy.

In the spring of 2011, we needed to hire a new assistant. Coach Morefield, who had been an important part of recruiting so many players in our early years, moved on. One of his main areas of expertise was relationships in the junior college ranks.

Grant McCasland was the head coach at a Division II school in Wichita Falls, Texas, and he had previously coached at a junior college in Midland. He'd also played basketball at Baylor in the late nineties.

When I first started reaching out to Coach McCasland, he was hesitant. He had heard from a few different coaches that we were cheating to get the players we were.

"Don't do it," several experienced Division I coaches told Coach McCasland. "You'll ruin your career."

Luckily, Coach McCasland was willing to talk with our staff, and I guess he liked what he heard. I also spent a lot of time talking to him. That's one thing about me—the more you tell me no, the more I want to work to get you to change your mind. I knew the rumors about us were out there, not just in the media but among some rival coaches. I mean, coaches are just like anyone else. When they get together, they're going to talk, and they're probably going to talk about the person who isn't there. As a staff, we never really spent much time hanging out with other coaches at group dinners after AAU tournaments or anything.

After the tournaments were over, we went back to our rooms to make recruiting calls and keep working. That's why we kept getting recruits people didn't think you could get at a school like Baylor. We worked for them. And if other people on the outside wanted to say something else, that was okay. But I was grateful Coach McCasland and other coaches who have decided to come work with us at Baylor were willing to take the time to get to know us. Because once they did, they knew the truth . . . and it was on our side.

By the time the 2011–2012 season was starting, the NCAA investigation was still looming over us.

My father had announced his retirement from Valparaiso in May 2011, with my brother, Bryce, taking over as the new head coach. Four months later, my father was diagnosed with prostate cancer.

Anytime you hear the word "cancer" with a parent, your heart skips. I trusted God, but that didn't make hearing my father was sick any easier to take. Three days later, it got worse. My mother, Janet, was diagnosed with stage 3 bladder cancer.

It's any person's nightmare. But it did give me a front-row seat to what faith in action can look like.

"It was obviously a shock, like a knife in the back," my father would say later. But after asking questions like "Why us?" my parents turned to their faith. "Janet is the rock, the foundation of our family, and she's very strong in her faith," my dad told the local newspaper when they ran a story on the diagnosis. "We knew this was God's will and he had a plan, so we prayed about it and prepared to fight it together."

Trusting in God isn't always easy. When a loved one is sick, it's never harder. But that doesn't mean God is any less in control.

My parents were lucky to have early detection and excellent medical care. My father was declared cancer free after having surgery.

> Trusting in God isn't always easy. When a loved one is sick, it's never harder. But that doesn't mean God is any less in control.

My mother didn't have it as easy. She had to go through chemotherapy and radiation treatments during our season that fall. But by the time the NCAA tournament rolled around, she, too, was cancer free.

My dad was honest, though. "I don't want to put any pressure on you," he told me. "But every time you win, it helps your mom."

Luckily, we'd had a lot of success on the court.

We started the season 13–0 and never really let up. Led by new JUCO point guard Pierre Jackson, we had five players average more than ten points per game, including Canadian sharpshooter Brady Heslip, along with Quincy Acy, Perry Jones, and Quincy Miller.

With that much balance, we won twelve conference games for the first time in school history and were ranked as high as No. 3 in the country. We even made it to the Big 12 championship game before losing to Missouri, and earned another 3 seed in the NCAA tournament. By that time my mother was feeling better than she had all year. I'd like to think we helped her, winning three games to make it to the Elite 8 for the second time in three seasons. We lost to Kentucky there, and they were definitely the better team that day. They went on to win the national championship, so once again we lost to the eventual champs in the Elite 8.

Being that close to every coach's dream of making a Final Four, only to fall one loss short in two of three years, was incredibly humbling. I wondered if God would ever give me, and our team, that blessing.

Luckily, remembering Philippians 4:6 to "be anxious for nothing," (NKJV) helped keep things in perspective. Yes, we'd come up short of a Final Four. But look what God had done! We won thirty games and had completely elevated the status of the program.

More importantly, we made some big spiritual strides. Perry Jones's mother was a lay minister, and she, Perry, and I spent the second half of the season texting and memorizing Bible verses together. That was such a blessing to be able to do with Perry and his mom.

Just like in basketball, where the best teams do the biggest things by getting the small things right—like footwork, spacing, passing, defense—in life, it's amazing the things you can accomplish spiritually when you just focus on the basics of reading and memorizing Scripture. Being in a small group with one of my players and his mother to that end was one of the highlights of my career.

It can be tempting to focus on the things God hasn't done in our lives. But doing so keeps our eyes in the wrong place. Look instead to what he has done. Celebrate that. By doing so, you experience the fullness God wants for all of us.

> **It's amazing how sometimes God can use the things we want least in life to help us the most.**

For me, that was easier to do because, in addition to our on-court success, my parents were getting healthy. Mom and Dad both seemed to be recovering well, and the doctors were optimistic. Plus, we were moving past the NCAA investigation. In their own way, those challenges had allowed me to focus on what really mattered. It's amazing how sometimes God can use the things we want least in life to help us the most.

TWELVE

ACCEPT HUMILITY, REFLECT PRAISE

My dear brothers and sisters, take note of this: Everyone should be quick to listen, slow to speak and slow to become angry.

JAMES 1:19

Coming off of our second Elite 8 in four years should have been an all-time high for us, especially considering that both times we had gone that far, the team that beat us eventually won the national championship. Unfortunately, because of the issues stemming from the impermissible texts and phone calls, I was forced to sit out the first two Big 12 games of the season.

It was a good reminder of the way God works. On the court we were in an unprecedented place. But if people can't look at your work and see God in it, how good is it really? This season, as much as any, helped remind us of that truth.

We had a lot of talent back, including Pierre Jackson at guard and front-court players Isaiah Austin, Rico Gathers, and Cory Jefferson. For whatever reason, though, we just couldn't seem to settle into a rhythm. We lost two of four games in a preseason tournament in Charleston, South Carolina, only to go into Rupp Arena and win at Kentucky. That win avenged our loss to them in the Elite 8 and snapped their fifty-five-game winning streak in their famous home arena. But then we came home and lost to Northwestern.

It just seemed to be like that for the entire season.

We closed out our nonconference schedule with another loss, although only by seven, at Gonzaga. With conference play starting, my suspension would begin. Our first two games were home against Texas and then at Texas Tech. Coach Tang took over as interim head coach and did an awesome job. He had our team ready to play, and our players were excited for the chance to give him his first win as a college coach. They beat Texas in overtime, with both Cory and Isaiah getting double-doubles and Pierre Jackson adding twenty-four points and six assists. Three days later we beat Texas Tech on the road by thirty-four, and I think Coach Tang was thinking there wasn't too much to being a head coach.

Honestly, though, I was thrilled for Coach Tang and our team. He was as much a part of the success of our program and its growth as anyone, and so to see him have the chance to lead the team, and for them to respond with wins, was as gratifying an experience as any I've been a part of. And the players were super happy for him as well. More importantly, we were playing up to our potential and seemed like we were ready to go on a run.

I came back for the third game, which we also won at home against TCU, part of our 5–1 start to conference play.

Then things went south. Quickly. We lost a close game at Oklahoma, and that seemed to send us in a downward spiral. From the end of January to the beginning of March, we lost numerous close games at home and a few not-so-close ones on the road. We'd been ranked as high as 16 earlier in the year, and now we weren't only not ranked; we weren't even in the "Others Receiving Votes" category. Our play and hopes were crumbling around us.

We went into the last game of the season, a home matchup against a top 5 Kansas team, in a major funk. We were in danger of missing the NCAAs, which after last year's run seemed like it would signal a major step back. Why was this happening?

I was sitting in my office, having a lunch that I wasn't very excited about and sort of sulking in the reality of my situation. As I thought about Kansas, my mind was stuck on how they had previously beaten us by seventeen at their place and looked like one of the best teams in the country. Truthfully, I was down.

The next thing I knew, there was a knock on my door and a man introduced himself to me as Scott Brewer, a pastor at a Dallas-area church and a character coach who had worked with Nations of Coaches. One of our staff members had asked him to come by and say hello.

"How you doing, Coach?" he asked me.

I just sort of shrugged my shoulders and went back to my meal.

I wasn't trying to be rude. I didn't know Pastor Brewer, and I was at a bit of a low point, and not just because I was eating a fast-food salad.

Pastor Brewer didn't need much of an opening.

"Coach, I don't know what God's doing," he told me. "I don't know what his plan is. I don't know if you'll win another game. But I know this: that human beings grow through adversity. And this is an opportunity for you to grow. And I know you love God, and God loves you. I know you love your team. And I know that you're trying to do this the right way. So let me tell you about adversity. I've lost a daughter, and to this day I don't understand why God asked my wife and me to basically give back to him something that he gave to us."

All of a sudden my problems didn't seem as big. This guy I just met hit me square between the eyes.

"We sold all of our possessions years ago and moved out to Los Angeles to plant a church," Pastor Brewer continued. "And thirty days after getting to LA, my wife was diagnosed with a stage 3 macroadenoma non-secreting tumor. And I remember driving on Santa Monica Boulevard East, headed toward LA by the La Brea Tar Pits. And I was angry.

"I said, 'God, we sold out for you. And this is the way you repay me.' But Coach Drew—" Pastor Brewer paused and looked me in the eyes. I was thinking about my daughter, and my wife, and I could hear both the truth and grace of God in Pastor Brewer's voice. "Coach, one of the best neurosurgeons in all the world at that time was at the USC hospital. And that man was the man that God called to take that tumor out of my wife's head. And at the time, I didn't know that was why God called us to LA. I didn't want to go to LA. I thought I must be an idiot for going to LA. But God knew that Dr. Weiss was there. God knew that Connie had a big tumor in her head. And you know what, Coach? Whether it's losing a child or hearing that your wife has a brain tumor, I'm a different person today and a stronger man today because of those two things."

My eyes started to tear up. He was right. These things are true about God.

"So here's what I know," Pastor Brewer concluded. "I know that in the midst of this adversity, God is trying to grow you and change you and transform you into his image. I'd like to pray for you. And if you don't mind, I'm going to get on my knees."

Sometimes we can forget about the amazing and life-changing power of Jesus, until we see someone use it in their own life. It's like seeing someone use a tool. Once you see what it can do, you can now see how that tool can be helpful.

Pastor Brewer was asking Jesus to help us.

This was the first time I had met this man, but I felt like something was happening. I got up, came around my desk, and got right next to him and put my arms around him. We were both on our knees in the middle of the office.

"God, I don't know what you're doing," Pastor Brewer began. "I know you've given this opportunity for Scott to grow and be challenged and that you want to transform him into a more powerful man and a stronger leader. And to that end, I pray that you will accomplish what you want to accomplish. I don't care what the papers say, I don't care what Vegas says, but I believe that Scott loves you, you love him, and he loves his team. And that you have a plan. And what I'm asking you for is that you'll do something special on Saturday."

> **Sometimes we can forget about the amazing and life-changing power of Jesus, until we see someone use it in their own life.**

When he said "do something special on Saturday," I squeezed his shoulders. I didn't know much, but I knew my team needed to hear what I just did. I looked at my watch.

"I need you to say everything you just said to me to my team. Their practice is in two and a half hours."

It was kind of a request. And it kind of wasn't.

Luckily Pastor Brewer could stick around. He had his son with him, who shot baskets in the practice gym to kill time while Pastor Brewer paced outside the Ferrell Center. He told me later he was just praying to God, saying, "God, I don't know these kids. Please give me the right words."

Well, he thought he was only going to be talking to our players. We had him speak to everyone. All the coaches, trainers, grad assistants, anyone I could find.

Pastor Brewer introduced himself and delivered the same talk to the team as he had in my office and ended by praying, on his knees, in the middle of the court. He ended the prayer with the same line. He said, "God, I don't care what the papers say. I don't care what Vegas says. I just pray that you do something special on Saturday."

He was the first pastor I'd ever heard reference "Vegas" in a prayer, but I think the message still resonated.

Two days later, we had a chance to see how much it did.

Kansas came into the game having won seven straight and knew they could win the conference title outright for the fifth season in a row if they beat us. But when their all-conference freshman Ben McLemore made the game's opening layup, that was the only lead they had for the game. Pierre Jackson scored twenty-eight points and Cory Jefferson had twenty-five, including hitting three three-pointers for the first time in his career. He'd been 0–7 all time before that. Kansas made it close in the second half, but we ended up winning by twenty-three.

For his part, Pastor Brewer had been at a wedding that Saturday. He said when he checked the score after and saw how big we had won, he was overwhelmed. And when he checked the box score, he joked that he could take credit for Cory Jefferson's three-point barrage.

It was an amazing performance when we needed it the most. Having finished 9–9 in conference play, we felt like we could make the NCAA tournament with a win in the Big 12 tournament against Oklahoma State. We had split the regular season matchup with them, so we knew they were beatable. And Pierre Jackson had just led the Big 12 in scoring and assists, the first player to do that in a Power Five conference since Jason Terry with Arizona.

We had a lot on the line and liked our chances, even with Oklahoma State being ranked No. 14 and being as talented as they were. Coming out of the gate, though, we seemed like we left our spirit back in Waco. The Cowboys jumped out to a twenty-point first-half lead, and we trailed by eighteen at the break.

We told our guys to stay calm, be positive, and just execute on offense. God can still do something special with our team. And when Gary Franklin's three-pointer went in and he was fouled with nineteen seconds left, allowing us to tie the game, it looked like God would. It was an amazing comeback led by Pierre Jackson, who had thirty-one for the game. But we fouled Oklahoma State with 2.9 seconds left and ended up losing by two.

After the game I told the media, "I feel like we can beat anybody in the country. If the committee sees us worthy, we would definitely be excited. That's an understatement."

Four days later, the committee decided we weren't worthy. We were headed to the NIT.

It was a disappointing outcome considering we had gone to the Elite 8 the year before. Plus, we had literally just beat a top 5 team by over twenty points, normally the kind of thing on a tournament résumé that, along with a .500 conference record, gets you in. But you always want to try to bloom where you're planted. You might not want to be there, but ask God to show you his reason.

God put us in the NIT, which meant, while not ideal, we still had a chance to be one of only two teams in the entire country to win its final game. All we could do was try. At this point we were establishing Baylor as a team that won games in the postseason. Just because it was a different tournament didn't mean we didn't want to win.

> **You always want to try to bloom where you're planted. You might not want to be there, but ask God to show you his reason.**

The good news was, as a 2 seed in the NIT, we got to host the first few games. Our team came out ready to prove they were one of the country's top teams. We beat Long Beach State by almost sixty, then pulled out a tight game at home against Arizona State. We beat

Providence in the Ferrell Center in the quarterfinals to earn another trip to New York for the NIT Semifinals.

For his part, Pierre Jackson was playing some of the best basketball of his career. He was averaging a double-double for the tournament and really showcasing the dynamic scoring and playmaking ability that helped us be so good the year before. Cory Jefferson and Isaiah Austin were also making big plays. And once we got to New York, they kept it rolling against BYU. We were up ten with about three minutes left, and I started to think, as a coach, maybe we could relax a little bit. Then this guy Matt Carlino, who looked like the second coming of Jimmer Fredette, started making threes from everywhere on the court. He was pulling up from well past the three-point arc and draining them. His last one bounced three times off the rim before falling in to make it a three-point game with thirty-eight seconds to go. Luckily, we made a free throw and then Carlino finally missed, allowing us to advance to the NIT Finals for the second time in school history.

I remembered us losing to Penn State in the NIT Finals in 2009 and reminded the players what it could be like to come so close and then miss out on the championship. It might not be the one we wanted at the beginning of the year, but it was there for the taking. We would have to beat Iowa in the championship. I was trying not to be superstitious about playing another Big 10 team in the finals.

Luckily, we had Pierre Jackson on this year's team. He scored 17 points and ten assists, and we won by 20. Isaiah Austin had 15 points, nine rebounds and five blocks, and Cory Jefferson had 23, though without attempting any three-pointers. AJ Walton, one of our seniors, had six steals in one of the best defensive performances I can remember. Our team celebrated like they'd won the NCAA tournament. Pierre was named the Most Outstanding Player for the tournament, and we had accomplished something that had never been done at Baylor: we'd won a title. In our tenth season in Waco, we had made history. Coach

Tang and I embraced after the game and just prayed in thanks to God for what he had done with us on our journey thus far.

In the postgame, the reporters asked how I would be celebrating. Noting I wasn't a big champagne guy, I told them the only thing in New York I had yet to enjoy was one of those famous hot dogs from a street vendor.

So, after the game, we rectified that omission. Our whole staff celebrated at a New York City street vendor hot dog stand. And, true to the reputation, it was one of the most amazing hot dogs ever!

But more than the hot dog, I enjoyed what I think was the lesson in God's faithfulness that I learned that season. I don't think it is an accident that the first championship we won at Baylor came the same season I had to sit out two games because of the self-imposed penalties. God can take us at our lowest point and turn it on its head. Not only did God help remind us, through Pastor Brewer's testimony, of what actual struggle looks like; he reminded us of his ability to use all of it.

Flying back to Waco, I thanked God for the lessons he always has for us to learn. None of us are perfect, and the Bible is filled with stories of people that God used and blessed, and then they forget about God's faithfulness or mess up in some way. I promised God to try to always be as faithful to him as he was to me, knowing that I could never actually achieve it but knowing that he would love me anyway.

THIRTEEN

SPREAD JOY

Whether you turn to the right or to the left, your ears will hear a voice behind you, saying, "This is the way; walk in it."

ISAIAH 30:21

One thing about me is I really try *not* to use the first person when talking about accomplishment. I'm not an "I" or "me" guy. There are a few reasons for this, but the biggest one is, God is in charge all the time. Like the verse in Isaiah says, regardless of which way you turn, God is there, guiding your steps and leading you along the path toward his perfect will. And so if I'm out there saying, "I did this," then it takes the focus off of God and puts it on me. And trust me: things will work out a lot better when God is the focus. As a staff, we've been fortunate to experience God's love and the power of the Holy Spirit in some really awesome ways.

Coming off the NIT championship was a real high, both professionally and spiritually. A lot of coaches don't necessarily give the NIT the same respect or acclaim as the NCAA tournament, and on some level that's understandable. But if you're going to give glory to God

123

for all the things he does in your life, your career, and your family, then that means celebrating all of it. So as a staff, we celebrated the NIT championship because God did that—and it was definitely a high point. And the following season would start out on a similar note.

We had a preseason tournament in Hawaii, which we lost in the championship game to Syracuse. I don't know why, but it's always easier to lose in Hawaii. But that loss to Syracuse was the only one we had in our first thirteen games, including a showdown with Kentucky as part of the Big 12/SEC classic. Kentucky came to Dallas ranked No. 3 in the country. We were ranked No. 20, but conceptually we were at home, since we were playing in the new AT&T stadium, where Jerry Jones's Dallas Cowboys played. I say conceptually because while the game was obviously played much closer to Waco than to Lexington, where the Wildcats are from, there was a giant ice storm the day of the game. It was early December, so the idea of a freeze wasn't totally out of left field. But because the ice was so heavy, our fans couldn't drive the two hours from Waco to make it to the game. As a result, only the Kentucky fans who either lived in or had traveled to the area for the game were able to make it to the stadium, meaning we played a game in Dallas in front of an overwhelmingly pro-Kentucky side.

As good as we were, with players like Royce O'Neale, Cory Jefferson, and Isaiah Austin, Kentucky had the advantage in terms of talent also. They had Devon Booker and Karl Anthony Towns (who went on to be the number one pick in the NBA draft the following summer), plus the Harrison twins and Willie Cauley-Stein.

They were loaded, and the Wildcat fans made themselves at home and made themselves heard in the big stadium. And it was a weird deal, because they made the court in the stadium like how they do for Final Four games, where the benches are down below where the players and the coach are on the court. So it was a weird moment for us as a staff because normally we are so collaborative and connected, and we are working together to call plays on offense or coverages on defense. But in this game, I was literally further away from my staff than I would be at just about any other time that season. We knew God had to be in control because we ended up winning by five.

As we entered Big 12 play, God remained in control, even though the winning stopped.

A lot of times, during some of the moments the world would consider to be the lowest, God brings you the closest to him, making those moments, in hindsight, some of the best.

After doing so well in nonconference play and entering the Big 12 portion of our season 12–1, we lost eight of the first ten conference games we played. Kenny Chery, our energetic point guard and team leader, got hurt, and we just couldn't find a way to compensate for his absence. David Chandler, a godly man who had been a trainer at Baylor since 1985, was working around the clock to help our players and program. But even he wasn't able to help get Kenny back on the court.

Kenny and the team were taking his injury and the losses really hard. Our energy was low, but our spirituality seemed even lower. As believers, we are supposed to find joy in knowing that God is in charge no matter what. Whether we turn to the right or left, God is guiding us. We seemed to be relying on ourselves for our joy, and we were routinely coming up empty. That was a problem.

The seventh loss in that stretch was a game at home, to Kansas. We lost by seventeen, and as I stood in the hallway outside the room where we meet with the media after the games, I saw Pastor Brewer walk by in the hallway. Suddenly I didn't care about the fact that our hopes of making the NCAA tournament were about over. I didn't care about how many more games we would win or lose the rest of that season. And I didn't care about any of the criticism that we as a staff were facing after losing so many games in such a short span of time. In that hallway, looking at the stats, none of it seemed to matter. I called Pastor Brewer over.

"We may not win another game this year, and I may be a horrible coach," I told him, "but if any of these guys leaves without knowing Christ, that will be the real loss."

Sometimes, when you find that you aren't having the success you want, ask yourself if what you want is what God would consider success. He's very clear: his goal is to be known.

> Sometimes, when you find that you aren't having the success you want, ask yourself if what you want is what God would consider success.

Our next game was at Oklahoma. In the lobby of the hotel the night before the game, Kenny Chery was talking with another of our guards, Brady Heslip, and our assistant, Tim Maloney. Coach Maloney, who had been a part of Athletes in Action, was a coach God wanted in the profession, not only because of his servant attitude and basketball mind but even more importantly, because he loved helping young men win the game of life.

Like Kenny, Brady is Canadian. Brady became a strong Christian who would lead Bible studies with the Canadian National Basketball team and was very comfortable talking with people about faith. As Kenny asked more questions about God and shared frustrations about things he'd been dealing with, including his ankle injury, Brady kept talking to Kenny about what it looked like to let Jesus be in charge of your life. At the beginning of the season, Pastor Wible's theme for the chapel services was "One," as in there's only one way to go to heaven. That night in a Norman, Oklahoma, hotel lobby, Kenny Chery told Brady Heslip that he wanted to let Jesus be in charge of his life.

It was the biggest moment of the season, and it didn't happen anywhere near a basketball court. The next morning, Kenny said he woke up in the hotel, thanked God for letting him wake up, and said he had a whole new outlook on life.

We lost the game in Norman. But it felt like we were starting to win the battles that really mattered.

After we got back from Oklahoma, we gathered as a group before practice. Our message focused on two things: we wanted to celebrate the amazing thing that Kenny had done, and we wanted to celebrate the opportunity God still had in front of us. Yes, we were 2–8 in conference, but we still had eight games to go. Typically, if you go .500 in conference play, you can make the tournament. So for us, that meant going 9–9, or basically winning seven of our next eight games. But as Pastor Wible reminded us, it wasn't just about a basketball game.

By this point, even though they didn't make it to the game in Dallas against Kentucky because of the weather, Baylor basketball had come to mean something to the people in Waco. We'd been to two Elite 8s and felt like we were giving our fans a team to be proud of because of what they said on the court, and hopefully what we showed them of our hearts. To drive home the point, Pastor Wible told a story about someone who went to his church. A regular attendee, someone who sat in the second row, had stopped coming to Pastor Wible's church after being diagnosed with a terminal illness. In visiting with the parishioner's wife, Pastor Wible learned that, while physically ill, the churchgoer's spirits were also down. His wife told Pastor Wible that he was a big Baylor basketball fan and joked that we hadn't been giving him much to get out of bed for.

Our next game was just a bus ride away, at TCU in Fort Worth. I don't know if it was the idea of our play having an impact on people's health, or Kenny Chery's newfound dedication to Jesus, or just that we made more shots and played better defense, but we beat TCU by thirty-three. It only improved our record in conference to 3–8, but it just seemed like something clicked. I was excited, but as much for the momentum we seemed to be developing spiritually as anything else. I told the team about something that happened to my brother, Bryce's team. Bryce was coaching at Valpo at the time. He had a player accept Jesus as his personal Lord and Savior before the game, and then the next game he went out and hit a ton of threes and helped them win the game. And I just told our players how amazing it was to see God bless that player and his team in a twenty-four-hour window like that. And how awesome it would be if something like that happened for us.

After our next practice, on Valentine's Day, Taurean Prince asked Coach Brewer if they could talk that night. A six-foot-seven sophomore from San Antonio, Taurean was one of our reserve forwards that season. Taurean had seen his minutes dip over the past few weeks and wanted to talk to Coach Brewer about his feelings about it, and just life in general.

Sometimes, when players that were highly touted in high school get to college and don't have the kind of immediate success they expected, it can impact them in some pretty dramatic ways. They might have put pressure on themselves to get to the NBA by a certain time and make money to provide for their families or themselves, and so when things don't seem to be lining up in that direction, it can be stressful and cause anxiety, depression, or other really challenging emotions.

Taurean had participated on an overseas trip for Athletes in Action that previous summer, so the idea of playing for God or letting him be in charge of your life wasn't totally new to Taurean. But he admitted to Coach Brewer that he was worrying about things he knew he couldn't control. He said he didn't want to be worried about things like that anymore and wanted God to be in control. So that night, with Coach Brewer by his side, Taurean asked Jesus to take control of his life.

Our second player had accepted Jesus in less than a week. That was the kind of winning streak we celebrated as a staff.

Our next game was at home against Kansas State. We had lost our last four games, which was the longest home losing streak we'd had as a team since we were able to field a full team. With nine minutes left, it looked like the losing streak might be extended. We trailed by ten. Then Kenny Chery, in his first game since accepting Jesus, took over.

On his way to a triple-double, Kenny assisted on our next two baskets, then scored two, then assisted on others. Down three with seconds left, Brady Heslip, our other Canadian who helped lead Kenny to Christ, made a three to force overtime. Kansas State was good—they entered the game 7–4 in Big 12 play—but our team could sense that our losing streak might be over. We actually ended up going to a second overtime.

Because the game was being extended, and we had other players in foul trouble and getting tired, we had to go down our bench. Taurean was now getting in the game.

In our first possession of double overtime, Taurean threw up a sort of wild shot from long range, and it banked in. A couple minutes later, Taurean had a dunk that drew a foul, leading to a three-point play the old-fashioned way. We won by fourteen in the second overtime, and Taurean finished with twelve points, his most in several weeks.

After the game, we were all happy for the win, but we were more awestruck by what God had done in and with our players. Kenny's ankle didn't bother him anymore. Taurean let God be in charge and he banked in a three. We knew trusting God's plan wasn't always easy. God was as good when we were 12–1 as he was when we started Big 12 play 2–8. But it's always good to celebrate when you see God do something. And that night, we saw it.

We won our next two games, but the biggest moment of the season came the night before we traveled to Austin for a game at Texas. We took a bus to Pastor Wible's church, Highland Baptist. We all filed out of the bus and into the sanctuary. From there, Kenny Chery, Taurean Prince, Royce O'Neale, Ish Wainwright, and Gary Franklin followed

Pastor Wible up to the baptistry tub and, one by one, were baptized in the name of the Father, the Son, and the Holy Spirit.

Amen.

So many thoughts went through my mind as we watched our players make the most important decisions of their lives. That was our tenth season in Waco, and while we had won an NIT championship and made it to the Elite 8 in 2010 and 2012, nothing seemed more important than what was happening in that moment. I was so thankful to God for putting me and our staff in Waco and giving us the coaches and players who helped create the conversations that allowed for an atmosphere where no matter which way you look, you'll hear the voice of God, however faintly. And I was thankful for Pastor Wible, the man who came into my office ten years ago and said he was our chaplain. And now, for the first time, he was baptizing Baylor basketball players.

> **No matter which way you look, you'll hear the voice of God, however faintly.**

We lost the game against Texas the next day. But somehow, that one didn't seem to bother us as much as it normally would.

After losing at Texas, we won the last three games of the regular season to finish up conference play at 9–9.

Before we started the Big 12 tournament, Pastor Wible gave us an update on the parishioner from his church who had taken ill. Apparently, after service on the previous Sunday, the churchgoer's wife had come up to Pastor Wible and asked him to come to the house and pay a visit to his congregant. When he arrived, Pastor Wible noticed the man was getting out of bed, taking meals again, and generally appeared to be in much better health and spirits than before.

"Well," Pastor Wible remarked, "what seems to have led to this change?" Pastor Wible told us that the man replied it was Baylor basketball. "They were dead in the water, and they had every reason to give up. They didn't, so I'm not going to either."

Going into the Big 12 tournament, Coach McCasland was in charge of the chapel services. He picked out the Old Testament story of Joseph, and for the week we were in Kansas City, before each game we talked about different aspects of the story of Joseph, leading up to chapter 41 of Genesis. Because in chapter 41, according to Coach McCasland, Joseph's story mirrored our story up to that point. A few chapters earlier, Joseph had been the favored son. When we were 12–1 and had beaten Kentucky in Dallas, so were we. Then tough times hit, and Joseph was sold into slavery. Then he was falsely accused by Potiphar's wife and was sent to prison. That was kind of like us, as Coach McCasland explained, dealing with Kenny's injury and starting conference play 2–8. But in chapter 41, Joseph was restored. He interpreted Pharaoh's dream, was elevated into Pharaoh's court, and eventually ascended to a place of prominence and authority. That, Coach McCasland was telling us, was what was in front of us.

Well, he was close.

We kept winning in the Big 12 tournament, beating TCU and Oklahoma in the first two rounds. We even beat Texas in the semifinals, putting us in our second Big 12 championship game ever. Once again, winning four games in four days proved to be a task too tough. We lost to Iowa State in the finals, but now knew we were a lock for the NCAA tournament.

Our first-round pod was in San Antonio. As a 6 seed, we beat Nebraska in the first round and then blew out 3-seeded Creighton in the second round. Winning by thirty in a game that sent us to the Sweet 16, in front of Texas fans—well, it had a restoring effect.

FOURTEEN

SURROUND YOURSELF WITH WISDOM

"For where two or three gather in my name, there am I with them."

MATTHEW 18:20

Basketball is a team sport, and that's true both for the players and the coaches. As coaches, we want our players to play together. We want them talking on defense and helping one another; we want them sharing the ball on offense and screening for each other and moving without the ball to make it easier for their teammates to make an assist or basket. And if they aren't playing, we want them to be an amazing teammate from the bench by cheering their teammates on and giving them energy.

That's the thing about basketball. Each person on the team impacts his teammates in profound ways.

That's true in life also. It's why God wants to be in every aspect of your life. Surrounding yourself with people who know him will spur growth in your spiritual journey in amazing ways.

As a coaching staff, one of the ways we try to model being good teammates is by doing those things ourselves. We try to coach as a team.

> **God wants to be in every aspect of your life. Surrounding yourself with people who know him will spur growth in your spiritual journey in amazing ways.**

There are a lot of responsibilities that a coaching staff must manage collectively. Someone has to run practices, scout opponents, set up the schedule, and recruit players, not to mention the million other things that pop up over the course of the day. There are many ways to make these things happen. Some head coaches do all the talking and leave the smaller tasks to their staff. Other coaches really delegate and let their assistants handle a great deal of the responsibility.

You'll probably never hear me proclaim myself to be the smartest coach in the room or act like I think I have all the ideas. The Bible says, "Don't go to war without the advice of others" (Proverbs 20:18, author's paraphrase).

I'm always very open to using things from other people if they will work. They say that coaching and preaching are the only two professions where it's okay to steal someone else's material. Well, as a coach, I'd much rather use a play that Billy Donovan drew up that I know will work than one I drew up that I think might work. I don't marry ideas because they're my ideas.

At Baylor, we coaches tackle everything collectively. We all scout our opponents. The assistant coaches all help me with practice. We all even share the responsibility for correcting and teaching. There are lots of benefits to this approach, in my opinion. One, because our players hear from a variety of voices, they are less likely to tune out the one from whom they're constantly hearing something they don't want to hear. Two, by giving all of our coaches greater roles, it expands their knowledge and experience base and prepares them to be head coaches themselves one day. I think this helps us in a few ways, in addition to demonstrating the value of being good teammates to our players. After all, many hands make light work.

This is really easy for me, because, ever since I've been at Baylor, we've had amazing assistants. And I don't just mean from a basketball perspective, although that's certainly true. The people who have worked with me to coach the players we've had in Waco have helped me grow as a teacher and leader on the court, but the impact they've had on me and our teams is so much greater than that.

It's always a good idea to surround yourself with people smarter than you and to hire people who help compensate for your weaknesses. I'm living proof of the benefits of that. So many of our coaches have been so mature spiritually, so much more well versed in the Bible, that it can't help but impact the people around them, starting with me.

We are constantly being shaped by the people in our lives. As a child, I was shaped and formed by God through my family's influence. As an adult, I'm shaped by the people I'm with and the things I choose to do. Surrounding myself with men who love God and seek him, and who also happen to be great basketball coaches, helps me in more ways than I can imagine.

A lot of people are happy to go to church one day a week. But how much sense does that make in a nutritional context? You can't eat one meal and try to last the whole week. At least I can't. I need a great meal for breakfast, then lunch and dinner. God's no different. He wants us to be fed all the time. So one of the best parts about our program being a ministry, and us as a staff being surrounded by people on mission for God that just happen to be basketball coaches, is we are constantly feeding each other. And I'm blessed to work with some amazing spiritual cooks.

One example of this is Jerome Tang.

When I first accepted the Baylor job, I had three different high school coaches tell me I should reach out to Coach Tang, who was coaching the basketball team and running the athletic department for Heritage Christian, a private school in Cleveland, Texas, down near Houston. Coach Tang was a pretty popular guy—his school had some of the top talent in the area, and so college coaches regularly reached out to him to ask about his players. The previous coach at Baylor had even talked to him about joining the Baylor staff, but when one of Coach Tang's players chose a different college, that offer disappeared.

When I showed up in Waco, I had a commitment from player Mamadou Diene, who was playing in Senegal but who possibly would have transferred to Coach Tang's school for a year before coming to Baylor. I told Coach Tang that I heard Mamadou would be staying in Africa but that I'd like to meet Coach Tang anyway. He tried to turn the meeting down and gave me every reason under the sun why I didn't need to meet him.

Luckily, one thing I'm good at is persistence and a willingness to chase someone hard once I believe he's the right fit.

Coach Tang was my first major recruiting win at Baylor.

We visited in Waco for nearly four hours. I was so impressed with Coach Tang's heart and faith, not to mention his basketball acumen. But as a new coach who was about to make a big hire for my staff, I didn't know *him*. And one thing you learn as a coach is not to hire people you don't know. But my dad told me, if I felt strongly about it, to invite myself to dinner at the Tangs' home, since that's a great way to get to know someone.

Now, Coach Tang was making $16,000 per year at Heritage Christian, and his wife had recently quit her job with the Texas foster care system because she was expecting their second child. When Coach Tang was visiting me in Waco, she had called to see if they would qualify for Medicaid. When she was told no, she sat in her car and wept.

As Coach Tang will tell you, he had $10.81 in his bank account. He spent all the money they had and fed me ribs. By the time I sat down, I could feel the love in the home, and I knew I needed to hire Coach Tang.

As I left the house, I told Coach and his wife, Rey, "The job is yours if you want it. But I can only pay you $70,000." We hugged and Coach Tang said he would pray about it. Right after I left, Coach Tang got a call from Leonard Hamilton, who had just finished his first year at Florida State and was recruiting one of Coach Tang's players.

"Coach Hamilton, is there anything I need to do?" Coach Tang asked. Coach Hamilton, a man of great faith, told him to get on his knees and thank God. Coach Tang dropped to his knees, prayed to God, and started weeping. He was on our staff the next week.

Shortly after hiring Coach Tang, I interviewed several candidates for an administrative assistant. Karen Craig immediately stood out because of her love for Christ and the joy she had in her heart. With a husband who was a former NFL player, she had joined him in ministry, and you could tell she had the Holy Spirit in her. While she was initially hesitant about accepting the job, she's been an incredible part of our ministry and a spiritual mentor to the coaches' wives, and also to our players. She's still the face of the program—she's the first person you see when you arrive at our office—and became famous for making players' favorite desserts for their birthdays.

Karen and Coach Tang weren't the only ones I had to recruit.

Paul Mills was working as a basketball staffer at Rice University in Houston when I first got the Baylor job. I'd been on the job for maybe a month and was working to get to know everyone in the area, so I went to Houston to speak at a coaching clinic when Coach Mills came up and introduced himself to me. Because he and Coach Tang had both been high school coaches in Houston, they knew each other, so after I spoke Coach Mills got my number from Coach Tang and called me, thinking he would just leave me a voicemail and offer any help with scheduling any games. Maybe, he suggested, we could get Rice for a game if we needed to play in Houston. Well, as a new coach who was trying to meet everyone all at once, I was living on my phone. So I answered his call.

We ended up talking for about an hour, and I just remember asking him so many questions. Again, I'm happy to gain knowledge from anyone.

"How do we recruit Houston?" I wanted to know.

"How do we recruit Dallas?"

"Can we ever beat Texas?"

I thought I was asking incredibly relevant and intelligent questions. Coach Mills thought I was a scatterbrain. As he told me later, he said he was thinking to himself, *This guy is all over the map. He has no idea what he's in for.*

After a while, I had one more question. "What do you make at Rice University?"

When I told him I thought we could pay him a little bit more if he would come to Baylor in an operations role, he said, "You're very kind. Thank you. But no."

As he told me later, he was thinking to himself there was no way he was going to take a job at Baylor less than a month after the news of the tragedy had dominated national news.

"Well," I continued, "I heard you were a Christian. Would you at least pray about it?"

"You know what? I will pray about it," Coach Mills responded. "But I'm 99 percent certain God will say no. So let me get back to you."

When he got home that night, he told his wife, "I just met one of the nuttiest guys I've ever spoken to in college basketball."

The next night I called Coach Mills and we spoke for an hour. Then I did it the next night. Then I did it for a fourth night in a row. I was just trying to get him to come visit us in Waco and see what we had going on.

The thing is, I've always believed in trusting God with the outcome if you put in the work. If I go all in on recruiting someone, and then he doesn't come, it's easier for me to sleep at night because I know God's in control. I know the Bible calls us to work. So I am happy to work in what I believe to be the pursuit of God's plan, and if it doesn't work out, then that's okay. But at least I'm going to give 100 percent and you'll know it!

I was giving it 100 percent to get Coach Mills.

Finally, he relented and agreed to come to Waco for a visit. Sort of. Turns out that Coach Mills was in charge of redoing the locker room at Rice, so he agreed to come to Waco but really he was just looking for ideas to steal about how to renovate their facilities.

As he would learn, some of the things we had on campus he couldn't steal.

When he and his wife arrived, we happened to have Calvin Miles, one of the top recruits in the state, on campus for a visit.

Man, Coach Mills thought to himself. *These guys have been on the job for a few weeks and they're already bringing in top recruits.*

We didn't end up signing Calvin Miles. But we did get Coach Mills. And with him, Coach Tang, Coach Brough, and Coach Driscoll and Coach Morefield—who had come with me from Valpo—we had our staff. None of us were over forty. We had no idea what we were in for, and we really didn't know what we were doing. We just knew we wanted to do it enthusiastically and asked God to be a part of it.

While our first few years weren't met with tremendous success in terms of our record, it wasn't for our lack of effort. We'd be working in the office until two or three o'clock in the morning, go home for a few hours, and then everybody was back in there by 8:00 a.m.

After our first year, we were putting conference championship banners on our office doors and just trying to vision cast for what we thought God could do at our school. The fact that we didn't win many games didn't diminish our spirits. We were on fire, partly because of our belief in the mission and partly because of our belief in the people we were on mission with.

Today, Coach Driscoll is the head coach at the University of North Florida. But for the eight seasons he was with us at Baylor, he will tell you that he grew spiritually because of the way he saw people like Coach Tang and Coach Mills live out their faith in their everyday lives. Along with Pastor Wible, those guys and I all did life together and were in community that pursued relationships with God. That's the thing about faith. Sometimes people just decide to give their hearts to Christ and it's like a switch, and they follow him for the rest of their lives. More often, though, people have faith, but they struggle with taking the next steps toward spiritual maturity. Coach Driscoll would say that working alongside Coach Tang and Coach Mills, he learned to be spiritually mature. We all did.

As much as anything else, that's the kind of cultural foundation that we laid in those early years. We set a standard for not just how we wanted the players to be but how we wanted the coaches to live. When you have genuine faith, you see service for and investment in others as things you get to do, not things you have to do. So when our assistant coaches started doing chapel services as part of the pregame routines on the road, while there might have been some initial hesitancy with some people, eventually God brought us to a place where we were all excited to share our faith.

It took a little longer for some of us.

Coach Alvin Brooks joined our staff from Kansas State in 2016.

A man of faith, he was attracted to the idea that he could live out his values and be open with his relationship with God as a coach at Baylor. But it almost didn't happen. He actually was going to accept a job with TCU but couldn't sleep well the night before it was to be announced. So he reconsidered and found his way to Waco. When Coach Brooks would later find out that his son was diagnosed with autism, he was thankful God had led him to a school that featured a world-class autism center.

> When you have genuine faith, you see service for and investment in others as things you get to do, not things you have to do.

The son of a legendary coach himself, Coach Brooks III was also an excellent recruiter and coach, so we were thrilled to have him join our staff. He just had one issue—he didn't want to do chapels.

Growing up in church, he'd always been taught to never talk about religion, politics, and money. So for thirty years he had been told not to talk about something, and then coming to Waco, we told him we made it part of our job to talk about our God. He would tell you that he was always afraid to share his faith because you never know what people's religion might be and how they may take it.

For our part, it wasn't a problem. I told him he didn't have to do any chapels if he didn't want to. But not everyone in his life agreed. Coach Brooks's wife challenged him. She said, "You have two small sons, and you don't want to be a better man?" Coach Brooks started doing chapels after that.

Now we call him Pastor Brooks. His chapels are amazing. He's one of the calmest speakers, so he sort of draws you in. But he'll tell you that before his first chapel, he was a nervous wreck. He probably called every pastor in the southern Texas area for advice.

But that's the thing about God. He can use everyone. And

everything. Some of the most powerful things that have happened with our team is the way some of our coaches used the toughest times in their lives to point back to God.

> **That's the thing about God. He can use everyone. And everything.**

Pastor Brewer started hanging out with our team in 2013, and his work as a character coach has helped directly lead people to committing their lives to Jesus. His story of losing a child and then dealing with his wife's illness, and trusting God with all of it, is an example of the height of spiritual maturity. However, he's not the only one on our staff who sees God's light in the darkness of our lives.

Bill Peterson has had a lengthy career as a skill development coach in the NBA. He's worked with NBA legends like Dirk Nowitzki and worked under incredibly successful NBA coaches. When he joined our team as director of operations, he immediately added value as someone our players know can help them take their games to the next level. But he does so much more than that.

Coach Peterson helps our players, and our staff, take their spiritual development to new heights because of his willingness to share the way he's seen God work in his life. Coach Peterson and his wife lost a daughter in a car accident in which Coach Peterson's father was driving.

A truck drove up from behind and rolled on top of Coach Peterson's father's car, killing his daughter on impact.

Not only did Coach Peterson and his wife lose a daughter, another daughter was in the seat next to her and suffered from survivor's guilt. And Coach Peterson's father was racked with guilt over any role he had in the tragedy.

"We had many anxious moments," Coach Peterson will tell our team. "Eventually my dad asked for forgiveness. And we—my wife and I—forgave him."

Coach Peterson had to deal with God too. "There were times that I'd drive back by myself from the airport, getting a recruit," Coach Peterson shares. "And, I'd stop and say, 'God, I don't understand how we're supposed to get through this.' But our ways are not God's ways. And I don't know why God took our daughter. But I do know she was a Christian. And my wife and I still believe in Jesus too. So God promises that we will see her again, in heaven. Until then, I just need to keep trusting God."

I can't tell you how meaningful it is for everyone on our team, from freshman walk-on to the head coach, to be surrounded by people who can share the stories and journeys of a faith like that.

Having a strong faith doesn't mean just celebrating the times God puts you on the mountaintop. Having faith is remembering that God is with you in the valley also. As a staff, we've been blessed to have people come into our lives who can share their faith in ways that resonate with people of all ages.

We spend a lot of time in practice on a variety of drills. We work on ball handling. We work on shooting. We work on rebounding positioning. And as coaches, our job is to show the team, and to instruct, on the proper way to execute all of the things that will make them successful on the court. But at Baylor, we spend as much time on our spiritual posture and positioning as anything else.

There's nothing more important that we can teach them. Winning the game of life is what matters most.

FIFTEEN

BE ON MISSION— WHEREVER YOU ARE

For it is by grace you have been saved, through faith—and this is not from yourselves, it is the gift of God—not by works, so that no one can boast.

EPHESIANS 2:8–9

Being a Christian in Texas, you hear a lot of amazing preaching and some amazing testimonies. I'm always blown away when I hear stories about people who walked through seasons of sin or just lived lifestyles that not only weren't pursuing God but maybe working in direct opposition to him, and then they meet Jesus and their lives are turned completely around.

The apostle Paul had a story like that. Born with the name Saul, he became one of the most prominent Jewish scholars and officials of his time. After Jesus' death and the early Christian movement began to take hold, Paul not only didn't believe it; he worked to persecute and execute people who claimed the Christian faith. Then one day, as Paul was traveling the road to Damascus, God grabbed hold of him and told him the truth. He temporarily blinded Saul. After explaining to him that Jesus was his true Son, God restored Saul's sight. From that point on, the Bible refers to him as Paul. God used Paul to spread the news of Jesus throughout much of the world. Paul's story is an amazing testament to God's ability to use anyone, regardless of their current situation, to accomplish his mission.

My story isn't quite as dramatic.

I was blessed to be raised in a Christian family. And I was raised by great parents. I accepted Christ in second grade, not because I was devastated by a life lived without him. I mean, I was seven. But I remember being in my seat in a youth church group, and they asked if any of us wanted to accept Jesus as our personal Lord and Savior and know that we would be able to go to heaven. I stood up. And when I asked Christ to live in my heart, I still remember feeling this burning sensation inside my heart. I felt changed. After I accepted Jesus, I tried to be an even better seven-year-old. But it isn't like I started giving sermons in the cafeteria.

I tried to obey the commandments, go to church, and live a godly life. In my family, it wasn't that hard. But it wasn't until I went on Athletes in Action trips as part of my coaching career when I was in my midtwenties that I think I saw and started to experience what it looked like to live out my faith in the real world. On those trips, I started to read the Bible and really develop a relationship with God. By reading the Bible, I saw how in the books of Galatians and Colossians, Paul (yes, that Paul) talked about the many ways we fall short of the glory of God. I may not have had a problem with drugs or alcohol or some of the other types of sins you hear some people admit to in their testimonies, but when Paul said envy, greed, jealousy, and lust were sins, I realized I needed all the grace I could get. Luckily, in the book of Ephesians, another book Paul wrote, he said that God knows we can't do it on our own. Ephesians 2:8–9 says, "For it is by grace you have been saved, through faith—and this is not from yourselves, it is the gift of God—not by works, so that no one can boast."

Up until that point, if I had died and God would have asked me, "Why should I let you into heaven?" I'd have probably told him because of my good works.

"See, God, I tried to go to church; I tried to obey the commandments; I tried to do the right thing. That's enough, right?"

I mean, in school you learn that everything is graded on a curve. So, if none of us can make it on our own, God's got to want some people in heaven, right? If you're one of the better ones, you have a shot because he's got to have somebody up there.

It wasn't until I actually spent time reading the Bible, being convicted by the evidence of my own brokenness and need for grace, that my faith really began to mature. And I realized that no matter how many good things I did, no matter how much I went to church, I couldn't earn my way into heaven. If it's left up to me, I'm going to mess it up with my own sinfulness.

I remember when I first heard about the Baylor job being open, I was out in Los Angeles at a coaches' convention. Coach Driscoll, who was in Los Angeles with me, knew Bill Carr, a consultant in college athletics and someone he thought I should get to know. Coach Driscoll, being an excellent assistant, arranged for us to have lunch the day we were flying back to Indiana.

The lunch went really well, and Coach Driscoll was excited and wanted us to get to the airport. I, being a generous and gracious guy, offered to give Carr a ride to the airport. Coach Driscoll wasn't a fan of the idea for several reasons, one being traffic, and the other being that sometimes you can spend too much time developing a relationship and it can backfire on you. He thought my youth and inexperience might become more apparent the longer we talked. But since Coach Driscoll was my assistant, we gave Bill Carr a ride.

Turns out, Coach Driscoll was right on both accounts. The traffic was pretty bad, and so it was kind of stressful on the way to the airport. As we sat in the middle of the freeway, with cars all around us, I looked over and saw, in the car next to us, the actor who played the one-armed man from the movie *The Fugitive*.

Well, you'd think that seeing a man who played a famous role in a famous movie might not be more important than trying to present a professional presence with a guy who might end up changing my career and my life.

You'd be wrong.

I started screaming to Coach Driscoll, "One-armed man! One-armed man!" and pointing frantically to the man next to us who was just trying to go about his day with, it should be noted, two hands on the steering wheel.

LinkedIn wasn't a thing back then, but if it had been, Coach Driscoll might have tried to update his résumé right there. He was mortified. This is exactly what he had wanted to avoid.

Luckily, Bill Carr was as big a fan of the movie as I was. He, too, shared my enthusiasm for seeing the actor. For his part, the actor, whose name is Andreas Katsulas, was fairly calm about it all and managed to give us a wave . . . with the arm that's missing in the movie!

The point is, that's what happens when I am in charge. I'm human and may well become overzealous and make a mess of whatever amazing opportunity God puts in front of me. That's why I need God's grace. We all do.

I think a lot of people get that part wrong. When you have that real relationship with Christ, and you turn your life over to him, yes, you'll still mess up. But if you get into the Word by reading the Bible, and you memorize Scripture, you'll find that God starts to take over. And you'll find that God will do so much more for your life than you ever could do on your own. I'm a basketball coach. I like to win. But I've come to understand that winning the game of life is the only game that matters. Eternity lasts so much longer than anything we might accomplish here on earth. There's only one way to guarantee you enjoy it. And it isn't through anything you can do by yourself.

There's an old joke about a pastor who dies and goes to heaven, and on the way to heaven, Saint Peter is at the gate. He greets the pastor and says, "Hi, nice to see you. I'm happy to let you into heaven. You just need a hundred points to get in. All you have to do is tell me about your life."

> **Winning the game of life is the only game that matters.**

The pastor, knowing he has lived his life in service to the Lord, relaxes right away and thinks to himself, *Hey, no problem.* The pastor says to Saint Peter, "Well, I've lived a moral life. I've been faithful to my wife, and we've stayed married for fifty years."

Saint Peter says, "Great job. You get two points."

The pastor is a little taken aback by that. He thought fifty years of fidelity might be worth a little more than that, but no matter. *Maybe Saint Peter wants to know that I was in the ministry,* he thinks to himself. So he tells him, "You know, I was a pastor in a megachurch for thirty years."

"Oh, that's fabulous," Saint Peter says. "Thank you for all your service and mature witness in what you've done. You've got five more points."

Now the pastor is getting nervous. Ninety-three points to go! *Maybe he wants to hear about mission work,* he thinks to himself.

"Well, you know, for ten years I was a missionary overseas, and I witnessed to people in remote corners of the world."

"Terrific!" Saint Peter says. "That's five more points!"

At that point, the pastor, somewhat defeatedly, says, "Man, the only way I'm going to get into heaven is by the grace of God."

"Bingo!" Saint Peter exclaims. "That's one hundred points. You're in."

The point is, you can't earn your way into heaven. Only by accepting the fact that Jesus paid that price for all of us can we truly accept the reality of our own brokenness. After all, there's only one perfect Father. And I think it's important that we as Christians are honest about it.

So many people don't come to Christ because they say they "don't want to be like the people in the church," or they "don't want to be like this person who says they're a Christian but then I see them behaving in a way that doesn't look like a life I want to live." The idea of a relationship with a heavenly Father seems threatening or unsafe. But that's why you can't look to humans. None of us are good enough. You have to look to God. He's the only One we can count on. Even our families, as much as we might love them, are people. And people, by definition, are broken. God has to be our rock. That's where it starts.

The Bible mentions about 2,390 names, at least in passing. God chose to mention that many different people as part of his story. Of those 1,000 were leaders. Out of the 1,000, there are only 100 about whom the Bible gives us sufficient data to get a full picture of their lives. And of those 100, only 33 of them finished well or ended up living their lives in a way that was pleasing to God. And those are the people in the Bible! Those are the ones whom God chose to tell us about.

The point is, everyone stumbles. But God knows that, and that's why he gives us grace through Jesus. The key is, don't let stumbling turn into failure. Don't stop walking with and running toward God. But some people do. That's failure. And most people fail when they should be finishing well! The apostle Paul wrote many of the books in the New Testament. In one of his letters to Timothy, another leader of the early church, Paul was actually in a prison cell in Rome, feeling like his life was nearly at an end and reflecting on the work the church still had to do and his role in it. In 2 Timothy 4:7, Paul said, "I have fought the good fight, I have finished the race. I have kept the faith."

That's what we have to do. And all we want to hear one day, when we have finished our fight, are the words Jesus shared in the book of Matthew. He was telling the parable of the talents, where a master went on a journey and gave three different servants different amounts of money to be stewards of while the master was gone. The first servant went out and took the five talents, according to Jesus, and gained five more. Matthew 25:21 tells us that when the master returned, he told that servant, "Well done, good and faithful servant! You have been faithful with a few things; I will put you in charge of many things. Come and share your master's happiness!"

That's how it is in life. God has given us all something. Pastor Michael Todd says Jesus has given us time, talent, and treasure. And that's what he wants us to use to serve him. And if we do that for our entire lives, that's finishing our race well.

During the Final Four I heard a testimony of a man who said he had gone to church his entire life and had just assumed he would go to heaven because he thought he generally lived a good life, went to church, and tried not to commit any really bad acts. But after he started to really develop a relationship with Christ, he'd realized that his mentality was wrong. Thinking you're going to heaven because of what you do, and not because of what Jesus did, is exactly backward. None of us can earn our way into heaven. We have to continue to pursue a relationship with God through the knowledge and acceptance of his Son's sacrifice for us all.

With God, you're either growing closer to him or you're going further away from him. If you are married and you want to stay married, you can't just ignore them after the wedding. You have to continue to court them. You have to continue to spend time with them. You have to continue to date them. It's the same way with God.

Now, I get that this part of faith is tough for some. For people who don't know God, the idea of "spending time" with someone you can't see or touch or have a conversation with in the traditional sense confuses them. It's understandable.

Here's the thing: if you do that, I promise you'll see God work in your life. For example, my memory is terrible. Legitimately bad. As I said earlier, Coach Driscoll likes to tease me that I have "selective memory" and won't remember things that I don't want to. But I'm here to tell you that even things I want to remember I often don't. It's okay. That's what God gave us Google for.

But here's the thing. When it comes to God's Word, I know probably fifty Bible verses off the top of my head, because God has put them in my heart. And that's only happened because I've spent time with God by praying, by reading the Bible, and by studying and talking about God in community with other people. That's how you pursue a relationship with and grow closer to God. You spend time in his Word by reading. You spend time talking to him by praying. And you spend time in community, in church, in small groups, in Bible studies, talking about him. And when you do that, I promise you God will change your life. And then, before you know it, you'll actually be in ministry too.

That's actually my favorite thing about what God has done with our team. He's blessed us, I think, because we aren't just a team. We are a ministry. Does that mean everyone on our team is a devout biblical scholar? As Paul would say, "By no means." But it does mean we are intentional about creating an atmosphere that pushes our players to be as strong spiritually as they are physically or academically. And we are up front about it in recruiting, so it isn't like people get on campus and are surprised: "Wait—you guys are Christians?"

But just because we are Christians doesn't mean the things God has called us to are easy.

One thing coaches always look at when they hire a staff is the family dynamic, especially the wife. Because in order for a coach to be successful, he has to be able to put in the time to be successful, and that means work-life balance can be difficult to find. A lot of people have families. But when you're a basketball coach, you don't just have your kids. You have your thirteen scholarship players, plus your walk-ons. And you also might have ten GAs and managers, so you have a small family you're responsible for, and the time that it requires to make sure you're meeting all their needs is a lot. Plus, you have to always be recruiting. Not only are you recruiting for the upcoming class but for the next two or three years out.

So when you host recruits, it's for a full weekend. And even when you aren't recruiting, most practice times for college Division I teams is three to seven o'clock because of the players' class schedules. Well, my own children have class schedules too, and then they have their practices for football or basketball or tennis around the same time. So being a coach and caring for the people you feel like God has put in your life has meant that I have missed football, I have missed basketball, I have missed choir, and I have missed tennis. I have missed a lot. And while I am so grateful for the mission I feel God has called me to, I'm clearly not perfect. Our ministry has impacted my wife and family in real ways. I pray God helps them see how they play a role in everything we do as a program and ministry. And I'm grateful that Kelly, who grew up with godly parents who happened to be basketball fans, has embraced her role as a coach's wife and everything it entails.

Everyone on our staff, and their families, have embraced and accepted their roles, and the sacrifice involved in our program. Because our basketball team is our ministry.

Everyone can have one. If you live your life on mission for God, everything you do can be a ministry, because everyone you encounter can be someone you serve because Jesus has served you.

But it wasn't always like that.

After we lost in the Sweet 16 to South Carolina in 2017, I felt like something was off. Even though we started off 15–0 and achieved the first No. 1 ranking in program history with Johnathan Motley, Ishmail Wainright, and Manu Lecomte, I felt like we could achieve more. Coach John Jakus joined our staff right after that season. He had been with Gonzaga, who had just lost to North Carolina in the championship game. Coach Jakus had coached with Athletes in Action, so he was actu-

> **If you live your life on mission for God, everything you do can be a ministry, because everyone you encounter can be someone you serve because Jesus has served you.**

ally a part of a basketball ministry. He'd also coached a professional team overseas but came back to the United States to make it easier on his family.

When he joined our staff, he helped us see how we could take things to the next level. For that next season, we had almost our entire roster turn over. We had to recruit nine new players, and Coach Jakus was one of the voices that told me he felt like we needed to get the work-life balance better. We were still doing all the things we'd always done.

We were preaching Christ, but maybe it felt more like work, and we weren't trusting Christ to play a role. We weren't engaging as much with the players, maybe we were talking *to* them more than *with* them. But our whole vibe just felt wrong. And as a result I think our on-the-court outcomes suffered. We started out the following year ranked but scuffled through and ended up losing in the NIT. It felt like we were spinning our wheels. And we were in this place where we were doing the program like everybody else. And then we just said, "We're not doing that anymore."

Ahead of the following summer, I committed that we needed to change. We had been about fellowship; we'd been about Bible studies and prayer. We'd tried to be about God.

It wasn't a time of repentance as much as a time of believing that God had something better out there for us and trusting in his plan enough to go look for it. As always, when you look for God, you'll notice he's easy to find.

SIXTEEN

SELL OUT FOR GOD

"But seek first his kingdom and his righteousness, and all these things will be given to you as well."

MATTHEW 6:33

In the off-season of 2019, I started reaching out to men of faith whom I felt I could learn from. We knew we needed to increase our pursuit of God and incorporation of Jesus into our program.

One thing I've long believed: God meets our needs before we know we have them. We just need to know where to look, and then be willing to see it as something that meets our need.

For me, I was able to lean on people I knew were head coaches of great faith. I called Dabo Swinney. I called Tony Dungy. They started to tell me about a culture of J.O.Y..

J.O.Y., they told me, stood for Jesus, Others, Yourself. Jesus needed to be in the front of everything, and it was our job as coaches to help our players see that.

That was a really dedicated summer. We brought in speakers constantly, whether they were from the outside or former NBA coaches, anyone we felt had wisdom to give us; we wanted to deepen our well.

THE ROAD TO J.O.Y.

Tony Gaskins was a life coach who worked with our former player Ekpe Udoh with the Utah Jazz, and one day he was in town and asked if he could come by. I said absolutely. He spoke to the players about accountability and how God is always watching everything we do. And, yes, we will mess up, but true spiritual maturity comes through the same, boring habits each and every day.

Our players are faced with all manner of distractions and temptations. Pastor Gaskins talked to them about going 1–0 in everything they do. Go 1–0 at breakfast by making a good decision. Go 1–0 at nighttime. Stack up enough wins, and before you know it, the spiritual season of your life will look like a winning one.

I think one of the big takeaways for me from that summer was, it all just happened naturally. We didn't force anything, but God put people in our lives and in our path that were able to speak truth in a way that fostered growth with all of us, including and especially me.

> **God put people in our lives and in our path that were able to speak truth in a way that fostered growth with all of us.**

We also started to recruit older players through transfers, feeling like more mature players might help us reestablish the level of spiritual maturity we were seeking.

We made it back to the NCAA tournament that season, losing to Gonzaga in the second round of the 2019 tournament. But it felt like we had made it back on the right path. That next summer we were eligible to take an overseas trip, which allowed us an extra ten days of practice.

Yes, we changed our defense while we were in Italy. And yes, we put in some new offensive sets and talked about basketball things. But more than anything else, we shared with one another stories of ourselves, of our faith, our fears and failures. Once again, only by fully leveraging the grace of Jesus, and how he magnifies our lives only when we fully deny them to ourselves, did we truly turn the corner.

Two of the most powerful moments from that trip didn't take place on the court and didn't directly involve any of our players. Three of our younger coaches, Aditya "AD" Malhotra, Ty Beard, and Jared Nuness, all took turns sharing their testimonies with the team. They actually shared their stories on the bus. But I know that had an impact on the players. All three are amazing servant leaders, and the players feel their authentic love for all of us. When you know that you are truly surrounded by a community of people who are pursuing God, it makes it so much easier for you to follow comfortably.

I think our reestablished cultural foundation of Christ-centered commitment made that trip, where we were isolated from our worlds and forced to connect in authentic ways, the cornerstone of the next two seasons.

One of my good friends in Waco runs a company that sells lettermen jackets. He is intentional about leading his staff meetings each day in prayer, and they have employee Bible studies. He doesn't separate his work from his faith. To him, they are one and the same. And God has blessed that business, not because God wants us all to be rich but because God has equipped my friend to be generous and has blessed the work that he does in God's name. As his business grows, he meets more people. And the more people he meets, either as customers or as employees, the more he can share the gospel.

I'm always impressed with people who are able to seamlessly blend their faith and their jobs in ways that draw more people to God. I've tried to do that in my life, and lately I've been blessed with a couple of people who have come into my life that I've been able to experience that with.

Rem Bakamus joined us as a graduate assistant a couple of years ago after being one of Gonzaga's most popular walk-ons. He was supposed to leave after the 2020 season, but because of COVID, he was granted an extra year of eligibility. Known for his man-bun and elaborate handshake routines when he was with the Zags, he cut his hair and toned down the bench activity for us. But he's still an amazingly fun young man.

Peyton Prudhomme won an NAIA championship with Texas Wesleyan in Fort Worth. After finishing his playing career, he joined us as a grad assistant too. Both Rem and Peyton worked incredibly hard for us, cutting up video, scouting opponents, and helping with our practices. But they both also started asking me, and our staff at various times, more about faith and the things I've learned along the road as a Christian and a coach. As they worked with us, you could absolutely see and feel how they were each growing in their faith.

Those are the best days in the office for our staff.

And the thing is, that's 100 percent not about me. I'm happy Jesus can use me in that way, but I was just the viewing screen. It's his movie.

That's my favorite thing about our team and program being a ministry. I grow as much as anyone during the season, because I'm around amazing coaches and players and in an atmosphere that we intentionally ask God to be a part of every day. We've structured our routine in ways that make time with God as common as a workout or a meal. Ironically, our coaches have all said that we feel like our healthiest spiritual times are during the season, because we are all together and so disciplined in our pursuit of God.

And I don't think it's a coincidence that as our discipline and commitment to God improved in our work lives, our team's performance improved as well.

In the lead-up to the season, we talked about what it would look like for us to try to implement the culture of J.O.Y. into our daily routines. So, how do you consistently put Jesus in front of yourself? Well, it starts by trying to encourage daily rhythms of prayer and Bible study, which we encouraged our team to do. And it also meant literally saying Jesus' name before you said anything else. So we started working with our team about giving what we called "J.O.Y. interviews," where when the media would ask them a question, they thanked Jesus, then their teammates, before they said anything about what they had done themselves.

It seemed like a simple thing, but the daily habit of denying yourself and elevating others and the name of Jesus can have a profound impact on anyone's life.

After all, the point is to become less so he can become greater. But it is not because God wants us to be diminished. If anything, he wants more for us than we can even imagine for ourselves. And only he can give it to us. That's why we put him first. It's our best shot.

Putting Jesus first in that overt way literally changed our program. We lost our second game of the season, in Alaska, against the University of Washington. It's a long flight from Alaska to Texas, but when you give up a ten-point lead in the last few minutes and lose by three, the flight doesn't feel any shorter.

I was frustrated but not discouraged. We felt good about our team and were committed to keeping Jesus in front, regardless of the scores. But it didn't hurt that after that game, the scores started going our way.

We won our next game, back in Waco, against Texas State, then went to South Carolina and won the Myrtle Beach Invitational, beating Villanova in the process. And when we got back to Texas, we kept winning, but each time making sure to stay committed to the concepts and principles we'd committed ourselves to. We sought out and talked about Jesus first. We played for one another, making extra passes, doing the dirty work that doesn't show up in a stat sheet, and cheering on our teammates when we weren't on the court. We were losing our individual selves and finding something greater than we could have ever gotten on our own.

We kept winning, and on January 20, 2020, we won our first ever game as the No. 1 ranked team in the country. We would eventually win twenty-three games in a row, which was the Big 12 record. We went ninety-four days without a loss. And while we lost a couple of games in the last few weeks of the season, we felt like we had our strongest team ever.

We were rolling and entered the Big 12 tournament as a projected No. 1 seed for the first time in school history, ready to show the world what we felt like Jesus had in store for us.

Like every other team's in the spring sports world, our 2020 season ended abruptly. The Big 12 tournament was canceled hours before we were supposed to play Kansas State in what would have been our first-round game. I know every team was disappointed to have their season end that way. But for us, after the run we'd been on, it felt especially frustrating.

All of a sudden, our identity as basketball players was taken away.

Luckily, our work to keep Jesus at the forefront of everything made losing the opportunity to achieve what we felt like God was leading us toward a little easier to take. We lost our chance to be champions. But we tried to appreciate the blessing of relying on God and not our own understanding.

That said, there were a lot of unanswered questions about what we would face the following season, if we even had a following season.

It was like a cliffhanger from an old soap opera, where the deep voice comes over the screen at the end with the outcome uncertain.

"Are Jared Butler, Mark Vital, and Davion Mitchell going to the draft?

"Is MaCio Teague turning pro?

"Will Freddie Gillespie and Devonte Bandoo come back for the extra year?

"Tune in next fall for the answers to these and more questions in . . . *As Baylor Basketball Turns!*"

When next fall came around, the possibility that we might not even play again made it all the more challenging.

SEVENTEEN

SEE BLESSINGS IN BUBBLES

*[Love] bears all things, believes all things, hopes all things,
endures all things.*

1 CORINTHIANS 13:7 (NKJV)

It's kind of hard to remember now, but in the summer and fall of 2020 there was a significant amount of debate over whether or not we would even have college sports that fall. The SEC and ACC had announced that they would be playing football no matter what. But the Pac 12 and the Big 10 had said they were not going to be playing football. Meanwhile, our officials from the Big 12 were debating.

This was a big deal to us because, as anyone who follows college sports knows, football always sets the tone. If our conference wasn't going to be playing football, we figured we wouldn't be playing basketball. So, this was concerning for a number of reasons, not the least of which was because, you know, we really wanted to play.

At some point, we heard that the Big 12 leaders were hearing from some medical people who would be recommending against playing due to concerns over myocarditis, or inflammation of the heart, as a long-term challenge to people who were infected by the virus.

I know in the post-COVID era, people can have a tendency to do their own research and come to whatever conclusion they want to. Well, as it turns out, we actually did have some experience with an actual medical expert in the area of myocarditis specifically. Several years ago we'd had a few players who went to go see Dr. Michael Ackerman with the Mayo Clinic. Dr. Ackerman is a world-renowned expert in these types of cardiovascular-related issues. Mack Rhoades, our athletic director, was able to get Dr. Ackerman's opinion on the issue of player safety and whether playing college sports would be feasible, and then eventually get him in front of the Big 12 officials, so at least they would have his perspective to consider. What a blessing that they listened.

Obviously, the Big 12, and eventually the Big 10 and Pac 12, decided to play. And thankfully, Dr. Ackerman and the other medical professionals who said that allowing college athletics would be safe were correct. But our road to the 2021 championship wouldn't happen without that decision in the fall of 2020. In a powerful and very spiritual way, I've felt that God ordained Dr. Ackerman to touch our players' lives years ago so that years later he could play a role in keeping college sports available.

Once we knew we would be playing, we felt like we had unfinished business. We'd been ranked No. 1 for much of the previous season. Why couldn't we get back there?

In one of our first chapel services of the new season, Coach Tang gave us a message that spoke to that. All the coaches sort of have chapel services that reflect the types of churches they go to. Well, Coach Tang's church is full of gospel music. So before the season, he played us a song called "Big" by Pastor Mike Jr. in one of his chapels. He asked the team to sit quietly and absorb the meaning of the lyrics.

"I believe, that it's my season . . . I believe, that it's my time . . . Breakthrough's in the room. It's yours if you want it. Anticipate it. God's getting ready to move."

As the music carried throughout our room, so many of the players had their heads down and their eyes closed in prayer. And it wasn't just the players. The staff was praying too.

"God . . . is working . . . a miracle . . . just for me . . . and it's gonna be . . . Big!"

So many of us had tears in our eyes and goose bumps on our skin. Coach Tang was telling us that, yes, the last year ended in a way none of us could have imagined or wanted. But as crazy as that was, God had something much bigger in store for us this upcoming season.

It was going to be Big.

And, true to Coach Tang's words, it was.

We started the season ranked No. 2 in the country. Only Gonzaga was ranked ahead of us.

We won our first three games, including in Indianapolis against Illinois. Actually, the team won their first three games. I only coached the Illinois game, since I had contracted COVID and had to sit out the first two while quarantining. Luckily, Coach Tang stepped up once again and led us to two victories. At 4–0 for his career, he is Baylor's only head coach with an undefeated record.

Next up would be a showdown with Gonzaga. Since we'd never beaten them, the idea of playing them in a 1 versus 2 matchup, was very exciting. All our players were amped. Then as we were getting on the elevator to head down to the game, we found out it was canceled. Gonzaga had some COVID issues on their team, and they wouldn't be able to play.

Immediately you start to wonder if the entire season would end up being canceled again. Gonzaga wasn't the only team dealing with those issues. Games were being canceled and teams were going into quarantine protocols all over the country. As a team, dealing with that kind of uncertainty was like seeing our previous season be canceled all over again. But all you could do was be patient. And pray. God was still in control.

In mid-December we had our own bout with COVID, causing our game against Texas to be postponed and a game with Tarleton State to be canceled. But we came back after ten days off and beat Kansas State by thirty-one and just kept rolling. We won our next twelve games to get to 17–0. It felt like last year's win streak, except we were still ranked No. 2 in the country, since Gonzaga had remained unbeaten as well. It seemed things were going exactly as they should. Then COVID struck—again.

> All you could do was be patient. And pray. God was still in control.

This time we missed three weeks due to several positive cases on our team. That's three weeks of not just not playing but not practicing, and more importantly, not experiencing the kind of intentional community we felt was so integral to our success.

I know most of the country went into lockdown during the spring of 2020, so they know what it was like to be isolated from the rest of the world, at least in some ways. But I think the toll that kind of isolation can take on you is even bigger if you are used to being in daily community with a specific group of people.

Whatever the reason, when we came back from the three-week quarantine, we weren't the same, on the court or off it. We just weren't as connected, and our play suffered as a result.

After winning a close game at home against Iowa State in our first game back, we went to Kansas and lost by thirteen.

That stung, because one of our goals the season before had been to win our first ever Big 12 championship. When we were winning twenty-three games in a row, we felt like we were on our way. But then as we started losing, we actually ended up second in the Big 12, behind Kansas.

After this loss, our players challenged themselves not to let this championship slip through our fingers. Like Coach Tang told us at the beginning of the year, God still wanted "Big" things for us. Doing them amid the uncertainty of a global pandemic would only make the things God was doing bigger.

We won a tough game at West Virginia, which was ranked No. 6 in the country, our next time out, in overtime, with Jared Butler scoring twenty-five points and handing out six assists. That seemed to remind us of what we were capable of. We won the last two games of our regular season, finishing with the school's first ever Big 12 regular season title. The only downside was not really being able to celebrate with all of our fans, who couldn't come to the games due to COVID.

We were humbled by what God had allowed us to achieve. But we knew he was capable of more.

Even after we lost our second-round game in the Big 12 tournament, we felt like we were ready to take the next step. We had never made it to a Final Four as a school, and we had never won an NCAA championship. This year, because of COVID, all the teams would be playing in the Indianapolis area, having to enter what the NCAA called a "Bubble." Major League Baseball and the NBA had successfully pulled off holding championships in neutral locations by limiting the places the teams could go and restricting the number of people inside the self-contained areas. The NCAA was determined to do it as well. We were allowed thirty-four people in our traveling party, which meant no families, friends, or nonessential personnel. We knew going into the tournament that it could mean some personal sacrifices, but they were ones we were prepared to make. And in some ways, we felt it actually played to our strength as a team.

Entering the Bubble meant being away from our families, friends, and loved ones. None of the coaches or trainers could see their children or wives. None of the players could see their girlfriends or parents. It was, by design, isolating. But at least we were isolated together.

At least for my family, there were some positives to the arrangement. Kelly and the children were able to be in Indianapolis for each game.

And us being in Indiana meant I had lots of friends, family, and former Valpo players who could come to the games. In addition, my brother, Bryce, was in his first year at Grand Canyon University in Arizona, and they made the NCAA tournament for the first time in school history. So my parents could come and watch both of us playing in the same city.

Bryce and I had both had teams in the tournament in 2017, but one game was in Tulsa and the other was in Salt Lake City, so they had to travel quite a bit. This year we were at Lucas Oil Stadium, where the Indianapolis Colts play, and Bryce was in the Farmers Coliseum, which was just down the street.

But I wasn't really focused on my family in the stands. I was locked into my family in the Bubble.

Some teams can play together on the court, but they aren't connected spiritually or culturally off it. Our guys came together inside that Indianapolis Bubble in ways that I think only made us better as a team, even when basketball was the furthest thing from our minds.

Yes, we had games to play, and we were able to take care of business in the first and second rounds against Hartford and Wisconsin. But we were only playing or practicing for so long. In the Bubble of our hotel, with only so many rooms to be able to share when we weren't in our own individual hotel rooms, we had to find a way to pass the time. And I think the way we spent ours in the hotel was as helpful as anything we did on the court.

From our athletic director, Mack Rhoades, to our graduate assistants and walk-ons, everyone had a role to play, and no one was any better than the person next to them. We all needed God. Everyone was an equal participant in our Bubble experience. And it was an experience.

To pass the time and keep things light, we played all kinds of games. My favorite was our Connect Four tournaments.

You know that phrase, "It's chess, not checkers"? Well, I think Connect Four is harder than both of them. It turns out that Davion Mitchell, our junior point guard, can see the Connect Four grid as well as he sees the court. He beat Mack Rhoades in an early round matchup that garnered quite a bit of attention from the crowd. On the court, we call Davion "Off Night" because whoever he is guarding is going to have an off night. In Connect Four he lowered the intensity, almost lulling his opponent into thinking he wasn't very good. But he was, in fact, very good. He won the entire tournament.

We also had an Uno tournament, which our sport administrator, Dawn Rogers, won. She constantly reminds us all about her victory. The players beat the coaches in our kickball tournament at a nearby field. Afterward, the coaches all needed treatment from our great trainer, Dave Snyder.

And we had a little fun at the players' expense.

One day, we called the players down for a team meeting. When they arrived, we had the coaches confiscate their phones and had all of them wait outside the meeting room. To add to the suspense, the players were told the coaches were upset with them. Then, at once, the players all entered the room to a singing group that consisted of the coaching staff, AD, strength coach, trainer, sports administrator, and the SID. Yes, the players walked into the room and we were singing a karaoke classic: "You've Lost that Loving Feeling." It turned into a fun karaoke night.

In a way, it was like summer camp. Stuff you do when you're isolated doesn't seem to make a ton of sense to the outside world. Like, you sing way more often at summer camp than you would in virtually any other place. But it just creates its own energy and culture, and it just sort of works in a way that brings everyone together. I mean, when you see grown male professionals singing Righteous Brothers songs alongside future NBA draft picks, it kind of makes everyone feel part of something bigger.

The thing is, our energy and camaraderie with one another seemed to be rubbing off on other people. The staff of the hotel always seemed to enjoy lingering around our team, and as they seemed to become fans of ours just from seeing our culture and antics, they enjoyed celebrating with our team each time we came back to the hotel with a win.

Not that it was all fun and games.

My brother, Bryce, had coached Grand Canyon University to the school's first NCAA tournament. They lost in the first round, but it was great to be able to be around him and his team. Four days after their first-round game, though, they experienced a tragedy.

Oscar Frayer, their star player and a senior who was about to become the first person in his family to graduate college, died in a car accident near his home in Sacramento.

We shared his story and journey with our players. He had actually just been baptized a few weeks earlier.

> **Tomorrow is promised to no one. All we can do is make the most out of today.**

"His eternity is secure," we told our team. "But as the Bible says, 'You do not know what tomorrow will bring'" (James 4:14 ESV).

We were heartbroken for Oscar's family and teammates. Tomorrow is promised to no one. All we can do is make the most out of today.

Our team seemed to take it to heart.

After our first two wins, we had several days before our Sweet 16 matchup with Villanova. While people weren't allowed inside our

Bubble physically, we had Charles Barkley, Robert Griffin III, and others talk to the team about different things via recorded videos.

I think the most impactful thing we heard in the days leading up to the Sweet 16 was from Greg Tonagel, my old point guard from Valpo. After his playing career ended, Greg had become a championship coach at Indiana Wesleyan University. He's now won multiple championships as a head coach, but more importantly, he is one of the most spiritually mature people I know.

A few years ago he spoke to our team about being fearless. As a program, we'd been to a couple of Elite 8s before. We'd been right there on the edge. But could we take the next step? Greg spoke to us about 2 Timothy 1:7, which says, "For God has not given us a spirit of fear, but of power and of love and of a sound mind" (NKJV).

That verse had actually been a theme of ours a season ago, and in fact is still in our locker room in Waco today. But the idea of having a fear, and overcoming it, was something that Greg encouraged us as a team to share about, to confront, and to overcome.

So as a team we decided on a powerful group exercise. We got together and we went, one by one, sharing something we were afraid of. To make others comfortable, I went first.

"I'm afraid that there will be a moment in a close game when we need the referees to look at a situation in our favor and because I'm not a big-name coach, because I'm not one of those yelling and cursing, because I'm not in the Hall of Fame, that *you* won't get the call you deserve. I fear that with everything on the line, my stature or demeanor will work against you. I believe that has happened before, and my fear is that it will happen again."

The room fell silent. For many it was a big moment that their coach would say words like that. But for me, honestly, it wasn't hard to be vulnerable with the team. That's one benefit of being in authentic Christian community. You can share with one another the ways you struggle and the things you struggle with. And then they can share with you the areas that they have a hard time with also. But the best part, and true power of being in God-honoring community, is that the people you are in relationship with can speak truth into your life in a restorative way. God loves us enough to meet us where we are, but he loves us too much to leave us there.

What happened after I shared is that the players and coaches in the room spoke their truth into my life. They told me that I was, in their eyes, a Hall of Fame coach, and God wanted us to win this championship. And that we were going to win this championship and he already had that ordained. Wow. The moment gave me so much energy.

> God loves us enough to meet us where we are, but he loves us too much to leave us there.

But as we went around the room, each person sharing a fear, the most gratifying part for me was hearing the players stand up for one another, and as one player shared a fear, others spoke biblical truth to encourage them. They cited Bible verses to back up their points. They demonstrated a level of spiritual depth that, for some of our players, was honestly shocking.

I love our players. I didn't know some of them were capable of that.

In many ways, the Bubble couldn't have been set up better for us. Our whole group, one through thirty-four, was there to invest in and pour into one another. People talk about roster depth—we went thirty-four deep in terms of quality, godly people who only wanted to serve one another. Our sports information director, David Kaye, was a military veteran who had donated one of his kidneys to help save his friend's life. Most of the team didn't even know David had done so until Matt Norlander, a writer at CBS SportsLine, mentioned it in a profile during the tournament. But to David, it wasn't that big of a deal. Our whole group was like that. And being stuck together like we were, we got to feed off of that energy and mindset the entire time we were in the Bubble. It was an amazing spiritual and competitive advantage.

We went out and beat Villanova—led by a Hall of Fame coach—by eleven, with Adam Flagler, our sixth man, leading us in scoring with sixteen. We played in Hinkle Field House, home of the Butler Bulldogs. They were my first "job experience" in college basketball. Now we were one game away from going to our first Final Four.

We played Arkansas, who as a 10 seed was on a Cinderella run and was led by their coach Eric Musselman, whose father was a long-time NBA coach and who had NBA head-coaching experience himself. Coach Brooks had the scout, and going into the game we felt like we had a good idea of what we needed to do.

We had been in the same hotel for several weeks. Our coaches could see their wives and children on Facetime, but that's not the same. Your iPhone can't give you a hug.

Still, there was no doubt what we were there to do. Even though a loss would mean seeing your loved ones that night, our love for one another was enough to keep us motivated. And our togetherness as a group was growing stronger. We had future NBA players in Jared Butler, Davion Mitchell, and MaCio Teague. But there was no sense of hierarchy. We all sang karaoke. And we all missed our families. We were the same.

Before the Arkansas game Coach Jakus did the pregame chapel. Coach Jakus's story is one of my favorites, and he shared it by contrast-ing the theme of J.O.Y. versus EGO. For us, J.O.Y. stands for Jesus, then Others, then Yourself. Coach Jakus took the letters of EGO and used it as an acrostic to spell out

Everyone exists for me
God becomes Santa Claus
Others exist for me

Before coming to Baylor, Coach Jakus had been a head coach in Europe, treating basketball as his ministry. He thought he was on track to become a head coach in one of the top European leagues. Instead, he ended up with a son who was diagnosed with autism, and so he moved his family back to the US to care for him. He also noted that as assistant coach at Gonzaga he had nearly experienced a national championship; the Zags lost that year to North Carolina. He shared with the team that instead of being upset that what he thought were his plans didn't work out, he was thankful that God led them to Baylor, where, like Coach Brooks, he could get his son specialized care at Baylor's autism center.

He ended the chapel by telling us all that if this was the moment he finally got to cut down the net, he knew Jesus would be on the ladder with him.

The moment his chapel was done, I went up to him and said, "Man, no matter what, after that, I know we are going to be okay."

We led for the entire game, jumping out to a 29–11 lead and holding on whenever Arkansas got close. But the thing I'll always remember about the time our team earned their way to their first ever Final Four appearance was how together we played. We had seventeen assists and twenty-five points from our bench. Our team, our entire team, had made school history and was on its way to the Final Four.

And our opponents looked very familiar.

EIGHTEEN

USE UNEXPECTED LOWS TO PREPARE FOR NEW HEIGHTS

"To whom much is given, from him much will be required."

LUKE 12:48 (NKJV)

In March 2020, right after our season ended and the world shut down because of COVID, Coach Brooks and his wife sat down and created a vision board. Having gotten the idea from comedian and TV host Steve Harvey, the Brookses wrote down and created a physical manifestation of the things they prayed that God would do in their lives.

Their board had several things on it. One of them was a Big 12 trophy, because that was a goal for our team and something that we had never done. Coach Brooks put the Final Four logo on there, since that was also a goal. And he had a picture of his father, Alvin Brooks Jr., who was the first African American head coach in any sport at the University of Houston, because Coach Brooks wants one day to be a head coach like his father.

What he didn't know was that before he got to be like his father,

Coach Brooks and our team were going to have to beat him because he was an assistant coach at Houston, our opponent in the Final Four.

Houston had been an emerging basketball powerhouse for several years. Coach Kelvin Sampson had done a great job with the program. As a 2 seed, they were one of the top teams in the country, with a deep roster that featured many different scoring threats, including two dynamic guards in Quentin Grimes and Marcus Sasser. Even when their All-Conference player Caleb Mills announced he was transferring after four games, the Cougars didn't miss a beat, winning their conference and coming into the game on a twelve-game winning streak. So we knew we'd have to be on top of our game to have a shot.

In the pregame chapel, Coach Tang talked to us about pride and how it keeps us from so much, including being the best versions of ourselves that God created us to be. To illustrate his point, Coach Tang shared one of his social media posts from inside the Bubble. Coach Tang had shared a clip of a recent practice where he was messing around on the court with MaCio Teague, and Coach Tang actually scored on MaCio. Now, Coach Tang is in his late forties, and MaCio is one of the best defenders we have. So Coach Tang was pretty excited. After he scored, he was running around on the court with his hands in the air, and he even slid on the court in celebration.

On social media a lot of people celebrated Coach's moment of glory. But not everyone. One of our former players, in a fun way, replied, "You traveled when you caught the ball. No basket."

"And what did I reply with?" Coach Tang told us. "I hit him back with 'Haterade.' I dismissed it. Because I didn't want to accept that maybe he was right. My pride wouldn't let me."

But after reviewing the video, Coach Tang said he realized he had, in fact, traveled. "Instead of me learning to get better, I deflected it," he said during chapel. "And that keeps me from being the version of myself God designed me to be."

It was a perfect message for our players to hear. We were about to play in our first ever Final Four as one of the top teams in the country. If we were going to beat Houston, we would have to humble ourselves and serve our teammates, making the extra pass, giving the extra effort, putting the team ahead of individual selves.

Our team carried the selfless spirit onto the court.

We had twelve assists in the first half alone, and that unselfishness helped us get some really open shots, which we were able to make. We made over half of our three-pointers and out-rebounded them 20–11 before halftime, which we entered up 45–20.

Normally, going into halftime with a big lead, while better than the alternative, can actually be a little dangerous. It can be easy for a team to relax and get complacent, taking their foot off the gas pedal, which can lead to the other team seizing the momentum and, if you aren't careful, getting back into the game. Luckily, Davion Mitchell wouldn't let that happen. He hit a shot just before halftime to put us up by twenty-five, and when he came into the locker room after doing a halftime interview the team was hooting and hollering over his performance.

He silenced them immediately.

"This game is not over!" he shouted.

Everyone stopped cheering and started focusing.

I can't tell you how important that is to not just our team but any group. When the guy who played the best and has the most reason to celebrate is the one getting everyone else to work the hardest, it's so powerful.

We went back out for the second half with the same energy we had in the first. Houston hit more shots, but we never backed down. We won by nineteen, with Jared Butler leading us in scoring with seventeen. Davion had eleven assists and no turnovers. Our whole team just played really well. We were now in the *National Championship* game!

We would play the winner of the UCLA-Gonzaga game, which was happening next.

There are few better feelings as a coach than watching a game to see who you'll play when you've already won your game. So as a staff, we were going to enjoy the next game no matter what. It just so happened that UCLA–Gonzaga turned into one of the greatest college basketball games of all time. It was close throughout, which was unusual for Gonzaga. Not only had Gonzaga not lost a game all season; they'd won their last twenty-seven games by double digits. They were up by seven in the second half, but Mick Cronin's Bruins didn't go away, eventually forcing overtime. With just seconds left and the game tied in overtime, Gonzaga's freshman guard, Jalen Suggs, took the pass from his own baseline, took a few dribbles, and pulled up at half-court. The ball was in the air as the clock expired, and when Suggs's shot banked in, Gonzaga became the first team since 1979 to make it to the championship game undefeated.

Suggs's shot was amazing. Gonzaga was even better.

We would have our work cut out for us.

In a way, it had to be Gonzaga. We'd never beaten them before, though we'd played them several times over the years. Coach Mark Few and I are good friends, and our teams had scrimmaged against each other in the preseason several times over the past few years. Coach Jakus was a former assistant for them too. And we were supposed to play each other in December, when they were No. 1 and we were No. 2. That game had been canceled because of COVID.

We were going to get to play this one.

The next day was Easter Sunday. As a team, we gathered together, knowing the next night would be our last in the Bubble regardless of the outcome. We might leave as champions; we might leave as runners-up. But no matter what, we were rejoining our community, and hopefully living lives that more closely reflected God's glory. During our chapel service, Pastor Brewer led us as we took communion. I never feel closer to God than when I am receiving the symbols of his body and blood, which were sacrificed for my own sin. We encouraged the team to take a moment of quiet reflection and just speak with God in their own hearts and minds in as honest a way as possible. This is not an overstatement: that moment of team communion will go down as a highlight for me no matter how long I live. How mature was our team in its faith? We had one player choose not to participate in communion because he said, "I need to get things right" before engaging in that sacred moment.

A day later we'd be playing Gonzaga, but we all have to face our own brokenness every day.

The next day, we were all business.

Because of his familiarity with the team, Coach Jakus was in charge of putting together the scouting report. As he reviewed the different players on the team and their tendencies and what we wanted to try to get them to do, our players seemed really focused. As far as indicators went, they seemed ready to play.

Our pregame chapel service was led by Coach Brooks, and the entire team was into it. The theme was "Raise the Rim." Coach Brooks had Mark Patterson, our six-foot-one walk-on guard, come out in front of a hoop we had inside the team conference room. The rim was adjustable, so Coach Brooks had it at the lowest setting.

"Mark, you're going to do three dunks," Coach Brooks told us. "And everyone else is going to judge you on the dunks."

So Mark came out and did the first dunk on a seven-foot rim. While he's just over six feet tall, Mark is pretty athletic. He swam and ran track in high school, so he jumped and then brought the ball between his legs before slamming it home. Even on a short rim, it was pretty impressive.

Then Coach Brooks raised the rim to about eight feet, and Mark took his second turn. This one was a 360, prompting further cheers and antics from the team. And Mark was loving it.

Lastly, we raised the rim to ten feet, and Coach Brooks told Mark to take his final dunk. At the higher level, Mark just did a regular dunk.

Then Coach Brooks asked us, "Which dunk was better? Who votes for the first dunk?" Most of the team raised their hands. "Okay. What about the second one?" Mark's 360 effort got a few votes. "And what about the third dunk?" Only Mark Vital said he liked that one the best.

Then Coach Brooks read from the book of Romans. Romans 12:2 says, "Do not conform to the pattern of this world, but be transformed by the renewing of your mind. Then you will be able to test and approve what God's will is—his good, pleasing and perfect will" (NKJV).

Coach Brooks told us that a lot of times in life our standards and the world's standards are so much lower than God's. We think we're killing it, going between our legs or doing a 360 dunk, but that's because we're playing on a lower rim. "God's standard," Coach Brooks said, "is always ten feet. So we have to know that. And we have to live accordingly."

Coach Brooks showed us his vision board that he and his wife had put together. Over a year ago he asked God to help us win our first Big 12 championship. God had done it. He'd asked God to help us go to our first Final Four. God had done that too. We even played Houston, the team that Coach Brooks had on his board in the picture of his father. God is amazing and can do anything. His plan for us is better than anything we can do for ourselves. But if we keep trying to dunk on the lower rims, we keep ourselves from reaching our full potential. We need to play on the tallest rim, the one God calls us to.

We knew the next game, the one we'd been waiting nearly two years for, was a chance to play on the tallest rim of all and realize the vision we felt like God had placed in our hearts.

NINETEEN

SLAY GOLIATH

*Do you not know that in a race all the runners run, but only
one gets the prize? Run in such a way as to get the prize.*

1 CORINTHIANS 9:24

For us to do that in the championship game, we kept it very simple
for our players. Win every possession. Go all out on defense, make
the extra pass on offense. Sacrifice for your teammates. Our players
seemed ready, but mostly they seemed really connected. That's what
gave me the most confidence. Throughout the Bubble, our team had
been excited to practice and excited to be around one another. We were
now in our third week in the imposed lockdown. That's three weeks
of only seeing your family on a screen or in the stands. Three weeks of
no hugs from our children or wives. But it had also been three weeks
of some of the best fellowship of our lives.

It was three weeks of regular Bible studies and prayer. Three weeks
of sharing and vulnerability and affirmation and accountability. In
some ways, it was three weeks of the closest thing to the early church
lifestyle any of us had experienced.

Each week we'd gotten closer as a team. And each week we'd gotten better on the court. Our players knew what had been taken from them last year when the season was canceled. No one *wanted* to be in the Bubble, really. But if it meant having a chance to make history, there were no complaints. In fact, our guys embraced it.

After chapel on championship Monday, I sent Mark Few a text. Mark and I had sent each other good-luck texts before each game in the tournament, and I thought this game shouldn't be any different.

"God, thank you for allowing Mark and me to have this Blessing. May both of us and our teams honor you with this platform tonight. Thank you that there are no losers tonight as we will be with you in heaven one day. Amen."

What Mark has done at Gonzaga is truly remarkable. He's one of the best people in college basketball, but he's also one of the best coaches. We knew it would take a truly special effort for us to be able to win. Gonzaga was undefeated for a reason.

We won the opening tip and went to work on offense. Davion hit Mark Vital on a screen and roll, and Mark put up a contested shot in the lane. It missed, but Mark didn't give up. He outmuscled the Bulldog defender for the rebound and then put up another shot. That one missed too, but Mark showed why he was "Mr. 95," our award that we give to the player who does the most extra things that don't get the attention they should. This time, Mark took the ball and passed it back out. We swung it out to Davion, who hit a tough jumper. It was just two points, but what we established in that possession was massive. Two offensive rebounds extended the possession. We were there to fight.

After Gonzaga missed a three, we came down on offense and Mark got another offensive rebound on MaCio's miss, then found Jared Butler cutting through the lane for a layup. On the next possession Davion drew a charge on defense, then came down and hit a three. We got another stop, and then Jared knifed his way through the lane for another layup. We were up 9–0, and Gonzaga was reeling.

More importantly, our defensive intensity was beyond excellent. Everyone wants to play offense, but defense is about desire, passion. Two seasons ago, because we were bringing in a class of smaller guards and wings, we switched from our traditional zone defense to a straight man to man. Coach Tang was in charge of installing it, and as much as anything else, I think our defense helped take us to the next level. Davion Mitchell is only six feet tall, but his energy and effort are immeasurable. A few days before the championship game, he was named the National Defensive Player of the Year, and tonight he was showing everyone why.

Sometimes in basketball, you can play good defense and the other team might still bank a shot in. Sometimes you can do everything right and make the extra pass and have a wide-open look and still miss it. You might be in great rebounding position, but the ball takes the odd bounce and the other team gets it. Those things can and do happen. They just didn't happen to us early on in this game. We hit shots, we got stops, grabbed rebounds, and worked our way out to a nineteen-point first-half lead. It was incredible, but I knew it couldn't last.

It didn't.

Gonzaga regained their footing and started playing like the No. 1 team in the country, and suddenly our big lead was cut to ten at halftime.

It's a coaching cliché to say basketball is a game of runs, but it's also true. It's amazing how quick someone can step to the line and miss a free throw, and then momentum just changes. Sometimes you miss a layup, or there's a blown call and then the other team comes down and scores. That's the one thing you're always looking out for as a coach: Has the momentum changed, and what can we do to change it back?

Going into halftime, the momentum was definitely with Gonzaga. In our locker room, our staff was frustrated. We'd been up nearly twenty, and now we felt lucky to still be up ten.

Normally at halftime, we coaches meet first and go over the stats and talk about what adjustments we might need to make offensively or defensively. And then we go into the locker room and present those adjustments to the players.

Sometimes, though, if the players come into the locker room frustrated and fighting among themselves, by the time we get in there to talk to them it's like a wildfire has started. And no matter how much you try, you can't really extinguish it. That can be toxic because if you come in and the players are not on the same page with one another, then you can spend the whole halftime trying to get them calmed down and to come back together. If that's what's required, then you aren't using the time to make the necessary adjustments, and then you just wasted your halftime. That's why it's so important to have great leaders in the locker room. With players like Davion, MaCio, Jared, and Mark, our guys stayed together.

Rather than being upset that we gave up as much of our lead as we did, we thought it was important to just emphasize the positives. We were still up ten. So our message to the players was, "We are twenty minutes from a championship. And we have a ten-point lead. Let's go win every possession."

That was really important for us because, while we as coaches had gone into the locker room frustrated, we weren't leaving it like that. I think that shift was important.

Jared Butler hit two threes right out of the gate to help us re-establish some momentum to start the second half. But Gonzaga was hanging right with us. The Bulldogs's Andrew Nembhard made a layup to make it a single-digit game with fourteen minutes to go. Excited for a good game, the crowd, as reduced as it was, got as loud as it could. The momentum was in danger of swinging back. It was the biggest moment in the game, and really in all of our basketball careers. We'd faced three weeks in a Bubble, a championship chase over two seasons, the uncertainty of a global pandemic, and now the undefeated, No. 1 team in the country was clawing its way back into the national title game.

Our team could have folded. We'd given up big leads in big games before in my career. But not this team. Not this year.

This team was ready to play on the tallest rim.

Over the next five minutes, we stopped their momentum and reclaimed our own. Mark Vital hit a layup. Jared Butler got to the line, and we extended our lead back to nineteen.

Gonzaga never broke, but they bent. We just focused on winning each possession. Don't worry about the score.

Eventually, Coach Tang came to me and tapped me on the shoulder.

"Should we empty the bench?" he yelled.

I thought he was crazy. *What?!* I thought to myself. *We're trying to win a championship, not make sure everyone plays.*

Our whole team was so focused on the game we hadn't noticed they were bringing in their bench players.

I gave him a look that let him know I thought he was nuts.

"Coach—they're emptying their bench," he calmly told me. "We can take a victory lap."

I remember we once played a game against Creighton in the NCAA tournament a few years ago. And we were up by thirty or so. And after the game Taurean Prince came up to me and said he had no idea about the score.

"I know what you mean about winning every possession," Taurean said. "I was just so locked in."

Those are the moments you live for as a coach. It's like when you're a parent, and your child does something not because a parent asks them to, but because they realize, "Oh, I know why you want me to do that. And it's important to me now."

That's when you feel like you've done your job. When your children, or players, cross the threshold and take ownership of the things you've been teaching.

As the clock wound down and both benches emptied, I saw the players celebrating on the bench and on the court.

Each year before the season begins, Pastor Brewer and I and our staff pray over the locker room, asking God to bless each individual player. We make notes and have specific things we hope for. Not related to basketball, but for their character, for their spiritual development, and for their personal growth. Some players battle self-confidence; some battle anxiety; some battle depression. Our players might be some of the best college basketball players in the country, but they're still young men. Over the past several years, they've faced every challenge you can imagine. And they've trusted God to help lead them through it.

As the clock wound down on our championship game and our time in the Bubble, I thanked God for the chance to be in their lives, and for putting them in mine. The players ran around and hugged one another, and as coaches, we were embracing also.

As we ran onto the court, Jim Nant, the iconic voice of college basketball and an authority on the tournament lovingly dubbed March Madness, offered a bold declarative statement to the nearly seventeen million people who had tuned in that night: "Coach Drew and Baylor have just completed college basketball's greatest rebound and rebuild with a championship!"

After the horn blew and the confetti started raining down onto the court, Jared Nuness, one of our assistant coaches, who played on the Valpo Sweet 16 team, grabbed Pastor Brewer.

"For eight years I've heard you pray that God would give us a national platform so that we would use it to honor him," Jared told Brewer. "Tonight, he answered that prayer."

I pray that as a program, we use the platform that God has given us to help point people toward what true victory looks like. I'm not sure I was mature enough to handle that responsibility earlier in my career. But God has shown me what putting Jesus and others before yourself can lead to. There truly is no more important thing you can do with your life, whatever you do for a living.

> I pray that as a program, we use the platform that God has given us to help point people toward what true victory looks like.

We happened to score more points than Gonzaga that night in Indianapolis. But I'd argue we'd won the ultimate championship a long time ago.

We waited around on the court while workers inside the arena assembled the makeshift stage for the trophy presentation.

Our national title was the culmination of the eighteen years I had been the coach at Baylor and the incredible challenges God helped us to overcome. It was the culmination of three weeks in the isolation of a pandemic-induced Bubble, which was life-altering in some inconvenient ways but also led to some of the deepest connections I'd ever had with players, coaches, and friends.

We were all thrilled to have won the game. But we were also excited because we were going home.

I'm not saying I wasn't grateful to hold the trophy. But that big gold ball wasn't the only thing I was excited to hug.

Standing on the stage, I was thankful to be surrounded by the people God put in my life to help me bring honor and glory to him. I tried to do that by being a good basketball coach. I tried to do that by being a good leader. I tried to do that by being a good steward of the blessings God had given me. And now Jim Nantz, the famous CBS announcer, was shouting a question to me that I couldn't even really hear because he was so far away and our Baylor fans in the stands were cheering so loudly.

We are all fully immersed in the Zoom era now, so we know what it's like when you ask someone a question and their screen is frozen and it's awkward because you don't know if you should reask the question or wait for a response.

Well, that's what happened to me on national television immediately after the biggest basketball win in our program's history.

We were on the stage, about to be crowned as the best college basketball team in the nation, a platform I had been praying God would give us to be able to talk about the amazing power a relationship with Jesus brings, and the only thing I could do was stare blankly at Nantz like my screen was frozen.

Quite the testimony.

"I know you can't hear me," Nantz said as he walked closer. He stepped a few feet nearer, spoke louder, and said, "Tell us about the start to this game."

"I can tell you our guys have been motivated all year," I said. "It's a player-led team. We're so blessed to have upperclassmen and leadership. But we play with a culture of J.O.Y.. That's Jesus, Others, Yourself. They came out, got off to a good start. And defensively, we are pretty good."

Yes, we got off to a good start. We played great defense; we hustled; we made some early three-pointers and then relied on our veteran players to help us maintain that lead. But we weren't winning that game, and we aren't winning where it really counts without our culture of J.O.Y..

As I told Nantz, for us, J.O.Y. stands for "Jesus, Others, and Yourself." And standing on that stage, that's exactly what I saw. By winning a title at Baylor, I saw a program that had been delivered from unconscionable despair to unimaginable heights. We'd arrived at Baylor amid one of the worst scandals in college basketball history. Now we had won the national title. God often uses the least of us to make amazing things happen, not so much to bless the vessels he chooses for the mission but so when people look and see what has happened, they have no choice but to see it as a thing God has done. God didn't use David to slay Goliath because he wanted more people to use slingshots. He wanted people to look down at the fallen giant, then look up to see an almighty God. Our team expected to win, so the David and Goliath reference isn't about them but about my journey. I was a pretty normal coach's son from a small town who couldn't have done a fraction of this without God. And standing on that stage and looking at the trophy they were about to give us, I was so humbled and excited to give him the praise for an epic story only he could have authored.

And then there were the Others.

Even though the confetti was literally flying in my face, I could still clearly see the players whom God used to help make Baylor's testimony known to the world.

I saw MaCio Teague, a finalist for numerous awards and one of four leaders of our team that season. MaCio had started his career at UNC Asheville because it was the only scholarship he'd been offered coming out of high school. He had transferred to us because he'd remembered we had recruited him and appreciated that we were honest with him throughout the process, even though we hadn't offered him a schol- arship. But by the time he got to Waco, he was ready: MaCio was one of the few guys to come to a Power Five school from a mid-major and not have his stats go down.

I saw Mark Vital, our senior guard from Louisiana, who was frustrated when he first got on campus because he had to redshirt. But that frustration led him to God and, over the course of his career, after several seasons of exploration, Mark was baptized earlier that season. Mark also graduated with the most Big 12 wins of any Baylor basketball player.

I saw Jared Butler. Well, I say I saw Jared. I did see him, in his oversized T-shirt and hat, hugging his teammates. But I also saw his journey to that stage. I had really wanted Jared to come to Baylor as a recruit. Not only was Jared a talented player, but he was also an excellent person, whose high school coach, and my good friend, assured me would add to the team on and off the court. But he'd chosen to go to Alabama over Baylor and Virginia.

Well, after getting to Alabama, Jared found out that he had a heart issue that Alabama's medical staff said made him ineligible to play. Or so they thought.

A few seasons earlier, we'd had a player, King McClure, with a similar condition, and as a result, we had sought out medical experts who had identified a treatment to allow him to play. King was a highly recruited player whom we were able to connect with one of the nation's leading cardiologists, and his success led him to serve as a role model for other athletes suffering the condition. Today, he's an announcer for ESPN.

About the time Jared was looking at transferring to Baylor, one of our players, Jake Lindsey, suffered an injury that made him take a medical hardship. While disappointing for Jake, it opened up a scholarship for Jared. Over the course of Jared's career, he developed not only as a player but as a person. His freshman year with us, he scored thirty points in a win at Kansas, and the first thing he said in his postgame interview was, "I want to thank my Lord and Savior, Jesus Christ." Spiritually, he only matured from there.

Jared led our team in scoring in the championship game. But the most impressive thing I can say about him is, today, I don't know anyone who is more on fire for Jesus. And that impacted our program in ways most people didn't see.

Throughout the course of the tournament, we had all witnessed the rise of Davion Mitchell. Davion started his career at Auburn and then transferred to our team after his freshman season. He'd sat out a year because of the transfer rules and then for the next two seasons emerged as one of the best players in the country. But that March he took it to a different level. Now, for some teams, if they aren't sold out on the idea of being about Others, having one player ascend can be a bad thing because one player's emergence can come at the expense of another's stats or playing time. But that never happened with us.

The better Davion played, and the more he started to get talked up as a possible lottery pick in the next NBA draft, there was never a hint of jealousy or anything less than enthusiastic support from his teammates. The night before our first Final Four game, when we had been hanging out in our Indianapolis hotel room for over two weeks, we'd gathered the team together and announced that Davion had been named National Defensive Player of the Year. Now, Mark Vital was also a finalist for that award. And it was Mark who stood up in front of the team and announced that Davion had won. "If I couldn't win the award, I want you to win it," he proclaimed in front of the group. No person could have showed more absolute joy while congratulating a teammate. As a coach, there is no better feeling than seeing our young men, led by Jared Butler and Mark Vital, who were so thrilled for a teammate.

That culture of J.O.Y. didn't happen by accident. And it didn't happen without a ton of help—not just from the people who were my teammates in leading our team but in leading our ministry.

From the stage, I saw the face of Jerome Tang, our associate head coach. We'd been together since our first season at Baylor. I reflected on how I'd offered him a job that night he'd spent all his money to feed me dinner, and now he's a national championship–winning coach who is more excited about how winning a title will elevate his platform for Jesus than his salary.

I saw the face of Mack Rhoades, our athletic director, and thought about how his taking the job at Baylor had really taken our pursuit of well-rounded student development to another level.

Under Mack, we made it a priority to live out our faith in our actions as much as we lived it out in our words. We established four pillars for character development for the entire athletic department, making sure we invested as much in their personal, academic, and spiritual development as we did in what they did athletically. We also had challenging conversations with our athletic staff, making sure they understood that at Baylor coaching was as much a calling as it was a job.

In 2018, as a result of lots of conversations with our athletics and university administration, we started a program called Baylor Built. It incorporates a holistic approach to character development, focusing on career and leadership development, personal skills, social responsibility, and community engagement, all while emphasizing spiritual growth.

Rhoades told me a story about how, two years ago, a significant donor sat down in the athletic director's office with a simple question: "Can we really win a national championship in football or in men's basketball and not compromise our Christian values?"

"Absolutely," Mack replied. "In fact, there's no other way to do it."

Amen.

At Baylor, we've worked intentionally to be aligned in pursuit of a God-honoring mission. We use that word a lot—*alignment.* And when you have alignment among leaders, among people, and you try to come alongside the work that God is doing, you can accomplish some unbelievable things.

Honestly, that's what was so special about this national championship. I'm not saying we were perfect, but those young men, along with our staff and administration, didn't compromise any one of our values. I think we won the title because we embraced them.

It took us eighteen years at Baylor, and me nineteen years as a head coach, to make a Final Four or win a national championship. Some people might have gotten down or disappointed about that. But I see God's hand in it. I don't think I was ready to be a national championship coach before, because I wasn't spiritually mature enough to use it in the most God-honoring way possible. I hope and pray that I have the people around me now to make sure we use this opportunity to make the most for his kingdom.

When you think of the things in your life as a ministry, instead of a career or a hobby, or even just a family, it changes everything. Our team, staff, and administration are sold out to the idea of being on mission for God and using the platform that being the best basketball team we can be gives us the opportunity to reflect that glory back to God.

> **When you think of the things in your life as a ministry, instead of a career or a hobby, or even just a family, it changes everything.**

That's what winning the championship meant to us. Jesus first, then others. Then yourself. Our team embraced it. Look what happened!

One of America's more famous pastors today is Louie Giglio. His Passion City Church in Atlanta routinely hosts tens of thousands of

THE ROAD TO J.O.Y.

people at conferences and retreats throughout the year. After we won the championship, someone sent me a link to his sermon from the Sunday following our win. It was called "Culture of J.O.Y.," and it was based on our team, and how we talked about Jesus and our culture in all the interviews we did.

Giglio defined the biblical concept of J.O.Y. as "gratitude, rooted in grace, regardless of circumstances." He contrasted it with happiness, which he defined as "an emotion based on circumstances and outcomes."

Listening to Pastor Giglio's sermon, which turned into a four-part series, I was overwhelmed not only with gratitude but with an abiding humility. I'm definitely not the first coach to win a national championship. And I'll never be confused for James Naismith. I didn't even come up with the name Culture of J.O.Y.. I got it from my friend Dabo Swinney, the national championship head football coach at Clemson University. He would tell you he got it from Tony Dungy, the Super Bowl–winning coach of the Indianapolis Colts. I'm not sure who he would tell you he got it from, but at some point someone *should* say he got it from Jesus. Because after all, that's what he taught. In his time on earth, we don't see any examples of Jesus doing something for himself. Everything was about serving others, regardless of their status in life, in order to glorify God.

In the weeks after the game, I thought about our players and how their joy hadn't faded even though the spotlight was off. And I thought about one of our favorite moments from the NCAA tournament, a moment no one else really saw. After games, we would go back to the hotel where they had this giant bracket that had every team in the NCAA tournament. Every time we won, we would take our name and put it into the next round.

Our team and traveling party had to take four buses to get back to the hotel, and the players always arrived first. But they always waited until the rest of the staff and assistants got back before they did it. As a player-led team, they also would pick someone to put the name in the next round that wasn't necessarily a star player. Oftentimes it was a walk-on who had cheered the loudest from the bench that game or a reserve who had given us a great spark off the bench. Watching them pick the right person each time to take part in that ceremony was like watching your children perform acts of kindness and getting it exactly right.

But it wasn't just our team standing around the bracket.

The hotel workers would all gather, and it became a tradition that when we got back to the hotel and got off the bus, the staff would be waiting on us and would cheer for us. They were genuinely happy for us and what we were accomplishing. And a lot of those hotel employees were graduates and fans of other schools. Even though they started the tournament cheering for a different jersey, they ended it cheering for us because, in seeing us interact with one another and them for the better part of a month, they had seen our hearts.

Then my mind came back to Pastor Giglio, and that series, and how from thousands of miles away he had been able to see our team's heart too.

I was just so incredibly grateful that God was using us to spread his message. And I'll always appreciate how, from inside of a Bubble, the light of Jesus shone through.

TWENTY

PARADE YOUR J.O.Y.

"You will celebrate all the good things that the LORD your God has given you and your family"

DEUTERONOMY 26:11 (NKJV)

There are many, many positive things that come with winning a championship. You receive attention and praise. You tend to get great interview requests on shows like *TODAY*, speaking or endorsement opportunities that can allow you to touch people you might not normally reach. You might even get the chance to write a book.

And you get to have a championship parade!

But if not managed correctly, all of those can also turn into negatives. Managing them in a healthy way became something our staff intentionally set out to do. We called all the stuff we had to do once we won the national title "championship problems." And trust me: we were glad to have them. But they still had to be done.

Attention and praise can be incredibly fun, but it can also lead to complacency. One of the things I did after the title game was reach out to coaches who had won championships—people like Mike

Krzyzewski, Billy Donovan, and Bill Belichick—to try to learn some wisdom from their experience as they worked to repeat as champions.

More opportunities to speak, or make public appearances, or earn extra money by being in commercials can also be positive. Anytime you have the opportunity to be blessed financially, it can equip you to be generous with other people, and that can be absolutely wonderful. But it can also become a distraction from what you need to be doing, the work that got us to that place where we could win a championship to be worthy of those opportunities. And it can be something that makes you think it's about you instead of the team or God.

In the pregame chapel before the Final Four game against Houston, Coach Tang gave an amazing talk on pride and how it can be what he called "the silent killer."

Pride is also a "championship problem." After you win a title, it can be easy to think *you* were the reason. We have talked a lot about King David over the years in our chapels. As a younger program without any history of success, it was easy to compare ourselves to David, who, as a boy, was chosen to defeat the much greater warrior in Goliath. And even though it didn't make sense to the world, David slayed Goliath through his faith in God. Lots of people know that story. We've frequently told it to our players. But David's story didn't end there, and neither does ours.

David went on to become king, and while he was a man after God's own heart, his reign wasn't without its stumbles. He committed adultery with one of his soldiers' wives; then he had the soldier, Uriah, intentionally placed in harm's way so he would be killed, leaving Bathsheba to David. He would later repent to God for those sins and be forgiven, though the consequences of his sin would linger. God still blessed David and gave him and Bathsheba a son, Solomon, who became a great ruler.

Despite what God had done in David's life—lifting him up in his battle with Goliath and forgiving him for some of the most grievous betrayals one can imagine—David still kept falling short of God's glory. Toward the end of his reign, as he prepared for a great battle, the Bible tells us David was tempted by Satan to count his army so that he might take pride in its size as opposed to trusting the Lord to help him prevail in battle.

Coach Tang told that story of David before the game against Houston, but I was thinking about it on that beautiful championship parade day as we walked down Austin Avenue in Waco. It can be easy to, as David did, count your army and think success is because of the resources that you bring to the table, not God. By definition, once David started counting his army, he took his eyes off of God.

Like David's after he beat Goliath, our story will continue also. Now we get to be the so-called kings of college basketball, at least for a little while. How will we reign? How will we handle the attention, the spotlight, and the opportunities that come with our accomplishments? It was important to our staff that, for the parade, we celebrate what God had done in the lives of our players, our coaches, and our program. We didn't want to count our army, though they would be marching down the street.

When it came time to plan the parade, we did what we felt was the best way to honor God and our culture of J.O.Y.. We put Jesus first, then others, then ourselves last. And that's exactly how we lined up in the parade.

We put Jesus first, then others, then ourselves last.

At the front of the parade, as always, was God. God had led us to where we were that day. God had delivered us from our own brokenness, both individually and as a program. Yes, the team had been complete disarray when we arrived eighteen years earlier. But the humble beginnings we'd inherited only served to heighten the greatness of what God has done in Waco. And for God, our story wasn't really that unique.

We had one player murder another, then some coaches lie about some of the details to avoid judgment and punishment. Cain killed Abel, then lied about it to God for the same reasons. We as people are too broken to deserve the rewards God promises us through a relationship with Jesus Christ. That's why his grace is so overwhelming. We need it to be.

From the back of the parade, I could see Jesus up front, because who else could take a group of broken people and turn it into this perfect thing? And, man, the parade was *perfect*.

Because of COVID, we hadn't been able to really play in front of or feel the energy from too many fans that season. But for the parade, they all came out. How perfect was it that the first time our players got to feel the love from our fans was after they'd won the championship?

Seeing so many people lining the street on the way to Waco City Hall was incredibly humbling. Our fans really are the best in America. Walking amid a sea of green and gold and hearing nonstop cheers for our players, it felt like we were in Lexington, Kentucky, or Tobacco Road in North Carolina. But we weren't. We were in Waco, Texas.

As soon as we'd won the championship and started planning the parade, our staff started thinking about how to really emphasize the "Others" part of our culture of J.O.Y.. Yes, this team had won the championship. But they hadn't done it in a vacuum. Romans tells us that God uses *all* things for his glory, and we really felt strongly that all the characters in the story of Baylor basketball had a role in helping us reach this perfect ending.

We did a few things. First, we had T-shirts made and put the names of all the players, coaches, and staff who had been part of our journey. All the names were used to spell out the word "FAMILY" across the chest. We had them made up after we won the Big 12, and a number of players said they wore theirs as they watched our national championship game. Then after we won the title, our graphics team put together a logo that we put onto shirts and masks and anything else that we handed out at the parade. In the logo, it had the "BU" letters up top, with "National Champions" underneath and fourteen stars to symbolize the fourteen players we had on the team. And on either side of that, we had the word "J.O.Y." on the left, with a checkered flag on the right, to symbolize the fact that we'd won the title in Indianapolis, home of the Indy 500. And then underneath that, we had a net for basketball. But we designed the number 99 into the net, which was a tribute to the ninety-nine players who had played for us in Waco since we arrived. All of our old players who saw that were really excited.

We also knew that Baylor basketball had been around for a lot longer than we had. We wanted to invite all former players to be in the parade. We didn't care if you played last year, ten years ago, or sixty years ago. If you were a former player, and you wanted to walk in the parade, you were welcome. And if you wanted to be in the parade but you couldn't walk, we had a golf cart for you. This is because these players had helped lay the foundation for our championship.

At eighty-six years old, Carroll Dawson turned down our golf cart.

He's probably most famous for being the general manager of the Houston Rockets that drafted Yao Ming in 2002, but before he was altering the global landscape of basketball, Carroll was a Baylor basketball player in the late 1950s and early '60s. At six foot five, he went to Kansas to play and would have been teammates with Wilt Chamberlain, but he returned to Texas instead and became an all-conference center. He also coached Baylor basketball in the 1970s before becoming an assistant with the Houston Rockets. In 1989 he was struck by lightning, which eventually caused him to move to the Rockets' front office, where he helped construct their championship teams. But he is a Baylor Bear through and through; his wife went to

Baylor, and he comes to as many events as he can. He was one of the most aggressive people on the phones when we told him about the parade, and he helped us line up a lot of the former players who showed up. But he insisted on walking. I figured, hey, he survived a lightning strike; he can probably handle a parade.

Jim Haller, who coached Baylor in the 1980s, also was really helpful in getting the word out to our former players. We had former pros, like Terry Teagle, Michael Williams, David Wesley, and Brian Skinner. But we had players who didn't go pro, like Matt Sayman and others from our first teams. We also had Dennis Lindsey, who played for Baylor in the late '80s and early '90s, who now works as an executive for the Utah Jazz. Dennis's son Jake was with him too. Remember: it was Jake, whose willingness to give up his scholarship after his medical issue, that allowed for us to be able to offer Jared Butler a scholarship.

In the parade, like in life, we are all connected.

That's why we were so excited to have the parade. Like at a restaurant: you're excited to eat the meal, but at least for me, the best part is the dessert. It's sweet. It's extra. It's amazing.

For us, winning the national title game was the meal. But the dessert was seeing all the former players there with their families. We had people who hadn't been back in a while, and they arrived with their entire families. And remember: a lot of other players hadn't had much success. Some of the players in our first years won fewer games in their entire careers than we won in just one or two seasons. For the Matt Saymans of the world to be able to walk the street and be cheered by crowds who hadn't shown up while they were playing was just so awesome. And, in a lot of ways, a perfect example of the kinds of things God can do.

Would our former players have preferred to have amazing careers and been able to play in front of massive crowds? I'm sure. But God's plan is always best. And one of the things I heard from the people ahead of us in the parade was how much more they appreciated the chance to experience the parade as an adult. Now they've done other things in life, and they get to come back as adults. Lots of our old players walked with their wives and with their kids. Lots of them had their grandkids and were able to explain to a different generation that they were a part of this awesome thing God had done.

Seeing all the players from the past come together, you kind of felt like you saw the physical embodiment of what the Bible talks about in terms of us all being part of one body. First Corinthians 12:12 says, "For just as the body is one and has many members, and all the members of the body, though many, are one body, so it is with Christ" (ESV).

The players from all different eras were the perfect picture of how we all have our own purposes and roles in the work that Christ is doing. Some people were all-conference players. Some people never left the bench. Some people made the NCAA tournament. Some people had seasons where they didn't even get to play a nonconference game. There were many different experiences represented by the people in that gathering on Austin Avenue, but they all were called to Baylor by the same God, and now his accomplishments were literally on parade.

Even the people who weren't there physically were still present in spirit.

Tweety Carter couldn't make it because he was overseas playing. Even though he was literally on the other side of the world, he couldn't have been more of a part of our body. Coach Jerome Tang's been in Waco as long as anyone, and we continue to benefit from his wisdom and passion. In fact, the only seasons we have ever won a championship were seasons in which he has served as interim coach for a couple of games. But coaches like Coach McCasland, who is now head coach at North Texas, and Coach Mills, who is now head coach at Oral Roberts, are all part of it too.

So the others, even the ones who weren't actually there, were ahead of us.

Then we had our players.

Davion Mitchell was still wearing his jersey from the game, which he insisted he hadn't washed. I didn't spend a ton of time next to him, but I kind of believe him. MaCio Teague and Mark Vital rode on the top, and I mean literally the top, of a convertible.

Jared Butler stood in the back of a pickup truck, holding on to the national championship trophy and waving it around. This was just months after the whole Tom Brady–throwing-the–Lombardi Trophy situation, so I was a little concerned. Luckily everyone made it to the main stage intact.

As a coach, I've been in a few parades in my day. But I have to say, walking the streets of Waco that April morning was one of the more spiritually rewarding experiences of my life. When Kelly and I arrived in Waco eighteen years ago, we were a young married couple just starting a career, really. There was so much unknown: how bad was the situation at Baylor? How much punishment would we get from the NCAA? Could we keep the players who had been on that team? Was I ready to be a Power Five conference coach?

The only thing we knew for sure was that God was good, all the time. We said yes to Baylor because we trusted God. Walking down the parade route was like walking past all the ways God had delivered on his promise. We walked past thousands of cheering fans. We walked with amazing players who had lived their lives in God-honoring ways and done amazing things on a basketball court. And I walked with not only my wife but now my three children, Mackenzie, Peyton, and Brody.

God has clearly blessed Kelly and me with a terrific family. But it goes well beyond our kids. Walking up that street, I was overcome with gratitude for how God put everyone in that parade into our lives.

When we made it to the front of Waco City Hall, we all got to climb up on stage and look out over the sea of green and gold. John Morris, our longtime announcer, emceed the presentation from the makeshift stage. He introduced Baylor's president, Linda Livingstone, who told us that as proud of what we had done on the court as the Baylor administration was, they were prouder of what we did, how we did it, and who we were off of it.

Then our athletic director, Mack Rhoades, got up and presented us, all of us, with the national championship trophy. "One of the most special things about today is that you get to share this amazing accomplishment with family," Mack said. "We have over 130 former players here to help celebrate this. Give them a round of applause."

The crowd went wild. It was, I'm fairly certain, the largest round of applause a lot of those guys have ever received.

Then they introduced me.

After almost falling off the stage because there was so much confetti and I couldn't see the ledge, I thanked God, the administration, the fans, and the players. Then I sat back down. It was the players' turn to talk, to celebrate with the fans, whom they'd missed for the past thirteen months.

After all, the players are the ones who do the work. Watching them take their turns, from walk-on to future first-round NBA draft pick, answering questions on the stage and celebrating the title, I thanked God for bringing them each into our team. And into our lives.

We had fourteen players on the championship team that year. And there were ninety-nine total players whom we'd had the privilege to coach. Our stories were all connected. Not just because we all played or coached for the same basketball team. But because we were all characters in a story God was writing. I was thankful for the way that particular chapter had played out. It's nice to win national titles. But God was just as good when we won five games for the season as he was when we won twenty-eight in the championship season. So I celebrate and appreciate the things that God allowed us to experience but also the people with whom he allowed us to experience it. I'm thankful for Kelly and our children. I'm thankful for my parents and brother and sister and entire family. I'm thankful for all the coaches and players whom I've learned from and who were willing to take a chance on whatever programs I've been working for. And I'm thankful for the amazing way God can write a story that brings so many people, from so many different places, together for one purpose.

As I had a bit of time to reflect on the emotion and grandiosity of the parade, a thought entered my mind. The parade was the culmination of an epic journey. My family and friends were there. Thousands of people cheering us whom we didn't even know we had impacted. So many of our former players, all of whom had a role in making us who we had become. Celebration. Laughter. Joy.

> **I'm thankful for the amazing way God can write a story that brings so many people, from so many different places, together for one purpose.**

This wasn't just a parade. It was a small glimpse of what heaven will be like.

And in his goodness, God gave us a sample of it that April day.

That is truly the most hopeful place I can end. Something as overwhelming and joyous as a national championship victory parade barely scratches the surface of what awaits us forever in heaven when our season on earth is done.

And as you close this book, I pray that this parade visual of heaven, our program's incredible journey, or something in our story points you to how good, how big, and how worth it God truly is.

AFTERWORD

By Don Yaeger

So I sent messengers to them with this reply: "I am carrying on a great project and cannot go down. Why should the work stop while I leave it and go down to you?"

NEHEMIAH 6:3

The fact that this And-One! even exists is because of Scott Drew. Not because Coach Drew fouled me, but because he thought it would be good for readers to have me share some of what I learned during his and my working relationship in bringing this book to you. Never have I had an author like Scott suggest such a thing. It just feels like an unusual but meaningful way to put a finishing touch to this story.

I've written more than thirty books with people from all walks of life. I've worked with amazing athletes like Walter Payton, Warrick Dunn, and Bubba Watson. I've worked with Hall of Fame leaders like John Wooden and Mike Krzyzewski. Never, in all my time as a writer, have I worked with someone who so relentlessly sought to serve others and deflect attention as Scott Drew.

In conducting the dozens of interviews that were part of the process of this book, one of the things I heard the most was, "When you first meet Scott, you kind of think it's fake. Like, how can someone be so nice for so long? And you eventually just wait for it to stop, and for the real Scott to come out."

Matt Driscoll said he saw it firsthand when they first arrived at Baylor. He said the players, freshly wounded from living through one of the worst scandals in college basketball history, didn't think these baby-faced Christians from Indiana could be for real. So they waited. Eventually, the team saw the same thing every day for long enough, and they realized what they saw was real. What they saw was a man in Scott Drew who was so sold out to his relationship with God that it motivated him to actually do the things it said in the Bible—namely, loving others as much as you love yourself.

What a concept.

I can understand what those Baylor players must have gone through, because my experience with Scott was similar. When I first agreed to work on this book with Scott and his wife, Kelly, I thought my assignment was to write a book about a basketball team. After all, Baylor had just won the national championship, completing what was called the biggest rebuild in college basketball history. Who wouldn't want to tell a story about a team and a program that went from staring down the cliff of the NCAA death penalty to celebrating at the top of the March Madness mountain?

What I soon realized, though, was that this isn't a book about a basketball team. It's a book about a ministry. This isn't really a story about Scott Drew. It's a story about God, and how a group of people have dedicated their lives to following him, and the things that have happened along the way. It just happens that Scott Drew was the leader of that group.

That actually presented one of the challenges in telling this story. Scott was happy to tell the story about the amazing things God has done in Waco. Except, Scott has this thing: he hates to use the words "I" and "me." Because he really does see other people first. The idea of the culture of J.O.Y., putting Jesus first, then Others, then Yourself, is lived out every day in the Drew household, and in the Baylor program at large. And it was lived out while writing this book.

Scott Drew gives Baylor athletic director Mack Rhoades a lot of credit for helping to instill a program encouraging of character formation into the entire Baylor athletic program. Drew believes that program helped push Baylor's teams to a higher level spiritually and athletically. But the stories Mack told me about Scott weren't really about how Scott conducts his practice or about how he emphasizes footwork in a defensive rebounding drill. They were about how, when Mack told Scott his daughter was trying to decide where to go to college, Scott had Mack call her up and put her on the phone. Then Scott went into an entire pitch, the same one he gives to basketball players, about why Mack Rhoades's daughter should go to Baylor. He also told me about how, after a big win or at a moment when Baylor was celebrating some new level of success, Scott would text his wife and tell her that she was just as much a part of the success because of the role she played in Mack's life and the entire Baylor family.

Like, who does that?

Grant McCasland was an assistant for Baylor from 2011 to 2016. Now a head coach at North Texas, McCasland's Mean Green actually upset Purdue in the first round of the NCAA tournament in 2021. So because McCasland's team was in the Bubble, he got to hang around the Baylor team and Scott for a while in Indianapolis. While North Texas's run ended, Baylor's continued, culminating in the trip to the Final Four. McCasland marveled to me about how, before the championship game, with a thousand other things happening in his world, Scott Drew would text him and see if he had tickets to the game and if he needed anything. McCasland spent five years with him as an assistant, so he saw Scott Drew up close every day. And he still can't believe what he sees. Not that he's surprised.

One of the more poignant stories Coach McCasland shared was from the 2014 season, when Baylor was coming off of their NIT championship and started the season 12–1. From that point, which at the time was the highest Baylor's program had ever been ranked and included a level of national attention that no Baylor team had ever received, the team went into a free fall, losing eight of the next ten conference games. We put that in the book, and Scott's take on the things he struggled with, both personally and spiritually, I think speak as much to who Scott Drew is as anything else.

But Grant McCasland told me about something Scott didn't share. He said that in that season, when the team was losing, and Scott and Kelly worried for the first time about their job security in Waco, Scott's mom was also struggling with cancer. The thing that stood out to Coach McCasland, though, was Scott's demeanor throughout the entire ordeal.

"I guess I remember uniquely that, here we are and our team is sucking, and his mom is dealing with this life-threatening disease. But Coach, I think in his own awesome way, didn't want to burden everybody else with it, which is him to a tee. He didn't want it to be something that would take away from what we were doing as a program and as a team. So weirdly enough, he was very private about his mom, but he was honest about it. He never allowed it to be a part of something that we felt like Coach wasn't connected to what we were doing as a team," McCasland told me. "He asked for prayer when we do our coaches' Bible study with the chaplain. So it wasn't like he was in denial about it. But I'll just never forget how consistent he was in his approach, and how he always made it about how to love other people."

In all the time I spent with Scott, he continued to make it about other people.

I think that's my favorite thing about this book. As a writer, it's my job to work with the subjects, hear their stories, and draw out the compelling parts and events that helped shape the narrative. And, for Baylor, there's plenty to talk about. But Scott's really only interested in telling one story—God's. Scott can connect the dots from how he was raised as the son of a basketball coach, who chose to pursue a lesser job so he could raise up his family in a godly way, to his own team's ability to lift the championship trophy and proclaim the name of Jesus on national television. Scott can see how God's hand helped bring the right players at the right time and how the talent of the players and their success on the court rose in tandem with Scott and his staff's own spiritual maturity.

And I have to tell you, being around someone who sees God in so many ways makes you start to look for him more completely yourself.

I had the privilege of writing for *Sports Illustrated* for a decade, and since then I've been fortunate to help some of sports' greatest figures tell their stories. But as I look back, God has actually been a part of many of those stories along the way. I've written with John Wooden, and he was among the most devout, humble men you could ever imagine. For a man with as many championships and accolades as he has, his happiest times were driving down the road with his daughter, singing along to praise music with the windows down and while the wonders of God remained just outside the door. I lived with Walter Payton for the last ten weeks of his life, as he fought the ravages of cancer in his final days. Walter faced his own death in ways that still inspire, choosing to use his legacy to promote organ donation. Talk about loving your neighbor.

I recently completed book projects with Bubba Watson and Rick Hendrick, both men who have come to a place where they tell the stories of their own accomplishments in the world of professional sports through the lens of gratitude for the things God has put in their lives.

For the longest time I thought of myself as a sportswriter. And then, somewhere along the way, because of the work I did with John Wooden and Coach K, among others, my career began to shift into documenting traits of leaders as well. I started a podcast that features people who have achieved success in the corporate world in part because of the lessons they learned through their own athletic careers. And then, a few years ago, I began to work with John Maxwell, the legendary speaker and author. Incredibly, I've now been asked to serve as someone to help carry on the kingdom-growing work that John and his team have started.

As I prepare to start this next phase of my career, I've realized that, in many ways, Scott's story parallels my own.

I grew up in Hawaii, raised as the son of a Methodist minister. We lived on Hawaii because that's where God took my father. There were worse places to grow up.

Like Scott, I went to college in Indiana, though I went to Ball State, while he went to Butler.

As my career progressed, and I went from working for newspapers in Texas to writing books and being full-time with *Sports Illustrated*, one of the first people I became close with in the sports world was Dale Brown, the longtime basketball coach at LSU. Dale actually hired Homer Drew, Scott's father, to be on his first staff at Baton Rouge when he took the job in 1972. And Scott credits Dale for encouraging Homer to hire Scott as an assistant on his Valparaiso teams when Scott was fresh out of school. Dale was best man in my wedding and is the godfather to both of my children now.

In some ways, I like to think this book is the merging of two paths. Scott's, which while in no ways perfect, has been spent largely in pursuit of excellence on the court and spiritual discipline off of it. And mine, which, in spite of my own shortcomings, God has managed to use for his own purposes.

Anytime you write a book with someone, you spend a lot of time either with them in person, or at least talking to them on the phone. Literally every time we spoke about this book project, and the ideas, themes, and people it would contain, Scott either started or ended the conversation with a prayer, asking for God's blessing for the project and for my time and family.

I don't think it's an accident that Scott and I ended up doing this book together.

I think Scott can see God's hand in all of it. I'm working on looking for it too.

I think my father would be proud.

ACKNOWLEDGMENTS

This is my first time writing a book. As a result, it is also my first time crafting acknowledgments for a book. It is a daunting task to try to make sure you are remembering to include those who played an important part in the story that you've been asked to tell.

With that being said, I must start out by acknowledging Jesus Christ as my Lord and Savior. Without Him none of this would be possible.

Second, I must acknowledge and thank my wife, Kelly, who has always been there for me as my partner and the love of my life. Without her by my side, and all of her love, wisdom, counsel, and sacrifices, there's no way I would have been able to spend the time or energy necessary to help be a part of building Baylor men's basketball. And I must also thank each of our children, Mackenzie, Peyton, and Brody, who have sacrificed so much as I have had to be away from them during so many important events and accomplishments in their lives. Things like practices, recruiting trips, away games, and speaking engagements all take time away from my family. But they still love me and cheer us all on, no matter what the scoreboard says.

I've always known the importance of a supportive family, as I saw that firsthand growing up a coach's son. I would like to thank my mom and dad, brother, and sister for helping shape and mold me into the man I am today. The love and support they've given me is unwavering and constant. I'm so blessed to have them in my life.

When you spend as much time working as we do, the people you work with become your family. I'd like to thank all of the people who have worked on and with our coaching staff:

Ty Beard	Grant McCasland
Alvin Brooks III	Shaun McPherson
Stephen Brough	Charlie Melton
David Chandler	Paul Mills
Dwon Clifton	Mark Morefield
Khalil Coltrain	Jared Nuness
Karen Craig	Sam Patterson
Matthew Driscoll	Bill Peterson
John Jakus	Dave Snyder
Aditya Malhotra	Jerome Tang
Tim Maloney	

Thank you so much for your time, energy, and sacrifices to help make Baylor basketball the program it is today. None of this would be possible if it weren't for you.

I also must thank all the players who have worn the Baylor jersey since we've been at Baylor:

Quincy Acy	Deuce Bello
James Akinjo	Roscoe Biggers
Darius Allen	Dale Bonner
Will Allen	Kendall Brown
Isaiah Austin	Aaron Bruce
Devonte Bandoo	Tim Bush

ACKNOWLEDGMENTS

Jared Butler	Curtis Jerrells
Tweety Carter	Tyson Jolly
Kenny Chery	Perry Jones III
Tristan Clark	Mario Kegler
Josh Clemons	Manu Lecomte
Givon Crump	Jake Lindsey
LJ Cryer	Josh Lomers
Jonathan Davis	Kijana Love
Deng Deng	Langston Love
Nolan Dennis	Stargell Love
Duran Diaz	Zach Loveday
Mamadou Diene	Logan Lowery
LaceDarius Dunn	Jo Lual-Acuil, Jr.
Henry Dugat	Carl Marshall
Fred Ellis	Makai Mason
Nino Etienne	Terry Maston
Patrick Fields	Matthew Mayer
Adam Flagler	King McClure
Gary Franklin	Robbie McKenzie
Al Freeman	Lester Medford
Rico Gathers	Quincy Miller
Freddie Gillespie	Austin Mills
Oscar Griffin	Davion Mitchell
R.T. Guinn	Wendell Mitchell
Corey Herring	J'mison Morgan
Hall Henderson	Jackson Moffatt
John Heard	Johnathan Motley
Brady Heslip	Jacob Neubert
Richard Hurd	Levi Norwood
Pierre Jackson	Obim Okeke
Cory Jefferson	Nuni Omot

ACKNOWLEDGMENTS

Royce O'Neale
Mark Paterson
Mitchell Paul
Taurean Prince
Ryan Pryor
Kevin Rogers
L.J. Rose
Chad Rykhoek
Austin Sacks
Matt Sayman
Dragan Sekelja
Mark Shepherd
Kevis Shipman
Carl Sims
Delbert Simpson

Tommy Swanson
Jonathan Tchamwa Tchatchoua
MaCio Teague
Flo Thamba
Djibril Thiam
Harvey Thomas
Terrance Thomas
Jordan Turner
Ekpe Udoh
Jari Vanttaja
Mark Vital
Ishmail Wainright
A.J.Walton
Kendall Wright

If it weren't for all your dedication, hard work, sweat, endless hours, and most of all effort for your brothers in Baylor basketball, we would have never become the program we are today. We are family for life.

I'd also like to thank all the Baylor administrators who have helped guide our university and athletic department that helped us create a culture of J.O.Y.:

Baylor University Presidents:
Dr. David Garland
Dr. John Lilley
Dr. Linda Livingstone
Dr. Robert Sloan
Judge Ken Starr

Baylor Directors of Athletics:

Ian McCaw

Mack Rhoades

Sport Administrators:

Nick Joos

Dawn Rogers

Sports Information Directors:

David Kaye

Heath Nielsen

Chris Yandle

To the voices of Baylor basketball, John Morris and Pat Nunley, thanks for all your endless energy to make sure the Baylor family can hear the broadcast of each and every one of our games. I'd also like to thank the media, both the local reporters and national ones, who have covered us and invested time, energy, and effort to get to know our program. Thank you for all you've done.

To everyone in the Baylor Athletic Department. Over the years you all have been such an important part of our success.

I knew this was God's timing for a book to be written on the culture of J.O.Y. and Baylor men's basketball. But as for many people, the thought of writing a book seemed to be intimidating and overwhelming. My collaborator, Don Yaeger, has been unbelievable in this process and he has made writing a book not only possible, but enjoyable, memorable, and fun. He did so in such a professional way that I believe anyone could write a book with Don's help. Don is also such a godly man, someone I am privileged to now call a friend, thanks to God's perfect timing and provision. His teammate, Eric Eggers, added so much value and spiritual depth. I am truly grateful for all your help in making this writing process work and work well.

I'd also like to thank my longtime agent, Sealy Yates, and his son and partner, Matt, who helped us pull this all together. You kept saying this story needed to be told, and finally that all came true. It certainly helps that Sealy is also a longtime Baylor man and that this book meant as much to him as a national championship.

I would be remiss if I did not thank our friends, Chip and Joanna Gaines, Doug McNamee, and the Magnolia team who have all been so encouraging by making this book a part of the Magnolia story.

Last, but certainly not least, I must thank Matt Baugher and everyone with HarperCollins Christian Publishing for their belief in this project. We knew you were the team that could deliver a final product that all of us would be very proud of, and we are!

ABOUT THE AUTHOR

Scott Drew, as head coach of men's basketball at Baylor University, led the greatest rebuild in college basketball history, guiding his team to its first National Championship and the first Big 12 title in school history. Entering his nineteenth season in 2021–22, Scott Drew is tied as the Big 12's longest-tenured head coach. His efforts have led to numerous coaching awards, including being named the 2017 Basketball Times National Coach of the Year and 2020 NBC Sports National Coach of the Year, as well as the Big 12 Conference Coach of the Year in both 2020 and 2021. Drew and his wife, Kelly, are the parents of one daughter, Mackenzie, and two sons, Peyton, and Brody. Follow Coach on Twitter @BUDREW.

Don Yaeger is an eleven-time *New York Times* bestselling author, longtime associate editor at *Sports Illustrated*, and one of the most in-demand public speakers on the corporate circuit. He delivers an average of seventy speeches a year to an annual audience of almost one hundred thousand. He and his wife, Jeanette, live in Tallahassee, Florida, with their two children.